Praise for
Life can be *This* Good

"More than a breath of fresh air, this book is a lifetime of deep breaths. Jan Goldstein is right on target. Life really can be *this* good. Receive this beautiful book with open arms—it is a gift to humanity."

—RICHARD CARLSON, author of
Don't Sweat the Small Stuff

"*Life Can Be* This *Good* is a book whose simple, direct, but subtle wisdom will enrich your life."

—RABBI DAVID WOLPE, author of
Making Loss Matter

"*Life Can Be* This *Good* provides a journey to the meaning and miracle of life's connections, a celebration of human possibilities, and a blueprint to awakening the spirit."

—JOHN GRAY, author of *Men Are from Mars, Women Are from Venus*

"Jan Goldstein weaves a magical blend of teaching stories and life lessons into a nurturing book we can all use in these troubled times."

—DEBBIE FORD, author of
The Secret of the Shadow

Life
can Be
This
Good

Awakening to the Miracles All Around Us

JAN GOLDSTEIN

Foreword by
RICHARD CARLSON

CONARI PRESS
Berkeley, California

Conari Press books are distributed by Publishers Group West

Book Design: Suzanne Albertson
Copyediting: Priscilla Stuckey

ISBN: 1-57324-803-7

LIBRARY OF CONGRESS CATALOGING-IN-PUBLICATION DATA

Goldstein, Jan.
Life can be this good : awakening to the miracles
all around us / Jan Goldstein.

p.   cm.
Includes index.
ISBN 1-57324-803-7
1. Conduct of life. I. Title.
BF637.C5 .G65 2002
289.7'2,—dc21

2001006805

Printed in the United States of America.

02 03 04 05   Phoenix   10 9 8 7 6 5 4 3 2 1

For my mother and father,
Roberta and Frank Goldstein,
who first taught me how *good* life
can truly be.

CONTENTS

Step Into...

Receive...

by RICHARD CARLSON,
author of *Don't Sweat the Small Stuff*

I sometimes refer to myself as a "realistic optimist." For as long as I can remember I've felt that, despite the obvious difficulties, imperfections, and even the pain and suffering, life is an incredible gift. To me, the possibilities are endless, and each of us has the potential for great joy. There's no question that life will rarely, if ever, be easy, but it can be magical, fun, entertaining, adventurous, and awesome.

A friend once remarked that life can be seen as a few dozen white dots against a background. The white dots represent the "highlights"—births, weddings, promotions, achievements, and so forth. The background represents the rest of it—day-to-day life. While most of us are tempted to see only the highlights as miraculous and exciting, the trick is to see the rest in the same light. The moment we do, everything changes. We realize that life can be magnificent and that it's a miracle that we're here at all. Everyday hassles take on less significance, and we stop sweating the small stuff! Ordinary life becomes quite extraordinary.

There are many stories of people who experience a "magical transformation" after a terminal diagnosis or shortly before death. Suddenly, life seems like an incredible miracle to them—every day and every moment are cherished. The good news is that there's no reason to wait to feel that way. We can do it now by simply changing and heightening our perspective. We can change our life for the better, not by changing our circumstances but simply by seeing life differently.

For the most part, my own hopeful and optimistic attitude toward life has been well received and somewhat contagious. When I am genuine and consistent in my own positive approach toward life, some of that positive outlook and energy seems to influence others. In the same way, when someone is happy, for example, it seems to makes me feel happier. When someone is calm, it makes me feel less anxious. The opportunity to feel how good life is can often be as available as a simple change in perspective.

I was honored and thrilled to be asked to write the foreword to this incredible and beautiful book. I consider Jan Goldstein to be a kindred spirit of mine. His soft, reflective approach toward living reminds me of the way I, too, want to live. His words uplift my spirit and help me take additional steps in the direction toward grace and gratitude.

Jan Goldstein is absolutely right. Life really can be this

good! And what's more, it's not a huge project to see it that way. In fact, it's quite simple. When you finish reading this book, you'll find yourself saying, "Of course." You'll see that optimism, gratitude, and realistic joy are natural ways to experience life.

Can you imagine what would happen if, even for a few minutes, the entire population had the sudden insight that life was a gift? We'd see less violence, hatred, and greed. Instead we would see people making each day all that it can be and creating a world full of compassion, loving kindness, and gratitude.

One of the ways to move in this direction is to read books like this one. I hope you enjoy it as much as I did. After reading it, I think you'll agree that life can be *this* good.

'Round the Storyteller's Fire

A man's boat capsizes.

A storm gathers overhead; lightning pitchforks the sky.

The man, whose name is Simon, being biblically literate and more pious than the Vatican, is unconcerned. As his arms flail to stay afloat, the crew of a schooner spies him from afar and makes for his rescue. Drawing closer, they bullhorn their intention to throw him a rope and pull him aboard. Simon waves them off, assuring them there is no need.

"God will save me. I'll be perfectly fine."

Despite the crew's protestations that he will surely drown, Simon, eyes scanning the heavens, fiercely insists they move on. They beg him to reconsider. The man of devotion, now spinning off prayers, remains adamant. Certain they've come face-to-face with a madman, the crew speeds off.

A short time later, bravely clinging to the ballast of a pitiful raft rudely forged from cases of Evian, Simon is startled at the horn of a cruise liner bearing down on him. Tossing out a life preserver, those on deck are astounded as Simon casts it as far from him as his strength will allow. A latter-day Ahab thundering at a bewildered crew, Simon rages through a spray of seawater:

"God will save me! *Be gone!*"

Twice more they throw him preservers. Twice more he rejects them. Unable to make headway, deeply concerned with the impending storm, the ship's captain steers for safer seas.

A short time later, his strength now ebbing away, Simon is suddenly revived by the sound of wings beating overhead. At last, his faith justified, he turns heavenward to behold one of God's ministering angels. A jolting disillusionment stiffens his bedraggled frame as the blade of a helicopter whips the air overhead.

A ladder is lowered. Simon, lifting his arms from the waters with Herculean effort, defiantly rejects it, shouting with a raised fist of blazing protest—

"*God . . . will . . . save . . . me!*"

As the helicopter hovers helplessly, Simon, with his last vestige of energy, waves it off with contemptuous finality. The helicopter turns as the storm erupts, speeding toward safety.

Simon drowns.

Arriving in heaven, the pious man rampages like a wild boar, madly gesticulating as he bears in on the throne of the Almighty.

"I was certain you would save me, and now I've drowned! Why didn't you come to my rescue? I waited for a miracle!"

Simon, waterlogged and defiant, stands dripping in righteous indignation, demanding an answer.

God clears his throat, ever so slightly bemused. "You wanted a miracle?" He begins softly, fixing his gentle gaze on the man.

"Let's see . . ." (He lifts his fingers to enumerate.)

"I sent a schooner.

"I sent a cruise ship.

"I sent a helicopter. . . ."

~

Sometimes it takes another who can point us to the gifts right in front of our hearts. Or to remind us of the good stuff we possibly once knew but have since forgotten. If you ask me, the first mistake Simon made was in turning his back on a simple maxim:

When sailing on the sea of life it's best to take a friend.

I'm glad you're here.

The Day The wind Had Its Say

I was at the lowest point in my life.

I had just become a single parent, with primary custody of

· 3 ·

my three young children. My heart was broken from the end of my marriage and, even more so, at the sudden ragged rip in the fabric of my children's innocence. And then, one week later, it got worse. My dad died.

I thought of changing my name to Job.

My little girl railed in helpless anguish. I wasn't sure how we were all going to make it. What I *did* know was that there was no alternative. Putting one foot in front of the other, we all began the process of learning to walk as a family all over again.

Months later, my mom took the kids for the first two weeks of their summer vacation. Practically throwing me out the door, she insisted that I go somewhere to heal. Which is how I ended up on the top deck of a ferry in the middle of a lake in Scotland, crying a river for my father, my children, and myself.

And it was there, in the midst of the sobbing and the water lapping and the loneliness of my heart, that I heard it.

It came to me as a whisper riding the wind. Was it my father's voice? My own? Didn't matter. It was perplexing and magical and utterly unexpected.

The voice spoke softly.

"Listen," it said.

I *was* listening. Believe me.

It spoke again with a gentle urgency. "Open," it breathed.

I was in a boat. How could——?

But before I could think another thought the voice insisted, "Step into . . ."

But into what? I hadn't the slightest idea.

And then, whispered like a benediction, came the final pronouncement: "Receive . . ."

The word vibrated on the water, shimmered, and was gone.

That was it?

Listen . . . Open . . . Step Into . . . Receive . . .

Not a lot to work with. If I was going to hear a voice in the middle of Scotland, the least it could do is speak in complete sentences.

But as I sat concentrating on the words that had floated to me on the wind, I suddenly became aware of the cry of a bird, primal and triumphant. And as the cry rent the sky above, something that had been sealed off unlocked within me. Lifting my eyes, I beheld the awe-inspiring flight of a hawk swooping across the lake. Without thinking, I rose to my feet, spreading my arms like wings, reaching up and out as if to embrace the sheer wonder of it all.

On the ride back to shore, still shaking with the thrill of the hawk, I felt stunned with a sudden realization. The voice I had heard, the whisper on the wind, had transmitted nothing less than a key for unlocking the riches of the universe. Not the supernatural variety, but those found in the natural world—gifts dropped in my path, waiting only for the awareness of my heart to bid them welcome. Like the hawk, and the voice, and the sudden recognition of what was right in front of my soul's door. Instead of mourning all I *didn't* have, I was suddenly infused with all I *did:* the miracle of my children, the spirit of my father coursing through me, and the knowledge that if I wanted to soar, well, birds and humans are related, after all, in some primordial and divinely attuned way.

I knew then I didn't want to be one more victim of life, bowed by the pain. I didn't want a heart that had been drained of hope, crammed with hurt and loss and an unspectacular desire to just get by. I wanted it filled with an eternal *yes.* With the power of the possible. And to do all this I needed to repair the strings inside me, strings that had been pulled and warped until I was out of tune.

Listen. Open. Step Into. Receive.

If I wanted to grow, spread my wings, connect to life's wonder, I had to begin to *listen,* to become conscious of what was happening all around me. Next, I would need to *open* myself to what I heard, to value it by creating space for it. This would allow me to *step into* experiences hitherto closed off to me, becoming part of their life-giving embrace. I would then be ready to *receive* and celebrate all the gifts that were coming to me, waiting to grace my life and all of our lives.

Riches both natural and abundant spin a web of magic around us every day. But, as so often happens in life's whirlwind of busy-ness, we are otherwise occupied. We have but to recognize them, see them, feel them, hear them, touch them, and allow them to touch us right back. It begins with the simple task of *awareness,* the process of allowing our inner instrument to vibrate with the music the universe is playing.

In that spirit, think of this book, its stories and musings, as a tuning fork for the heart. These are true-life accounts of people and places I've encountered and perspectives I've acquired interacting with the gifts that have come my way. They are pockets of life's poetry that have fashioned a space in my heart. I pass them along with the hope they will similarly touch yours.

I have centered these thoughts and anecdotes upon each portion of the blueprint I received in mystic wonderment the day the wind had its say. As you marinate in each story, search within you for the stories of your own life that resonate with a similar truth. I hope this book will lead you to unlock rooms within yourself that you may not have entered in a long while. In sitting with each account, may you find not only the affirmation that life can be good, but also the conviction that each of us has the power to make it *this* good. How good is that?

So good that we bless each day for its possibilities.

So good that we find, in the small corners of our lives,

bountiful riches that let us know how wealthy we really are.

So good that we recognize that in searching for the meaning of life, we are led back to our soul's door through which all that is truly meaningful flows.

～

Around the fires in the highlands of ancient Scotland would sit a storyteller, a person whose purpose it was to entertain and illuminate. I've always fancied myself a bit of a Scotsman, what with family connections on my mother's side. And as you and I have come to learn, there's wisdom to be found in company, so . . .

Listen.

Open.

Step Into.

Receive.

～

Come . . . Let's build a fire.

Listen…

The jungle speaks to me because I know how to listen.

Mowgli, in *The Jungle Book* by RUDYARD KIPLING

Life Can Be *This* Good
When We Listen

The world intrudes with noise and obsessions. The drums of life beat a cadence, and we scramble to keep time.

As adults, we sometimes lose our ability to hear what the universe is saying, its message drowned out by the roar of technology, the blare of commercial ballyhoo. The gifts working their way into our lives often whisper in vain. We cannot hear them, we say. Or if making out the sound, we cannot decipher the message.

It has not always been thus. As children, we warmed to tales and adventures that were read to us. We traveled the highways of imagination. We greeted reality with wonder. We listened for it—in the rainfall on a summer's night, in the heartbeat of our mother as we lay against her chest, in the morning song coming from the bluebirds outside our window.

We were meant to hear the world with the ears of life's celebrants. We can find our way back to that ability to truly listen. What we once heard, we will hear again. And more.

Listening is a step to consciousness, toward recognizing who we are and who we were meant to be—beings around whom the fire of life crackles with possibilities.

Tune the instrument of your heart to hear, and the song of life will vibrate ever more richly through you. The wonder you deserve will begin to flow to you.

And in the quiet of your soul you will make out plainly the message the universe is sending: *you* are a miracle.

Life can be *this* good.

Finding our own song

Childhood, for me, was like sailing on an ocean of wonder.

Maybe it was my dad's passion for theater. He fulfilled his dream of becoming an accomplished actor, making his debut in professional theater in his forties. Perhaps it was the lyrical nature of my home. My mom was, and is, a poet. While I was still a kid she had six books of her verse published and was honored nationally. During my childhood, imagination ran rampant in my home, and I was its lucky companion.

I can still see the doll I would rock and dress and put to sleep nightly. That's right, a doll! Who knew then that years down the road, I would rock and sing and tickle the backs of my children, putting them to sleep in almost exactly the same way as I did the little doll of my youth. (I outgrew this phase after the age of seven, but until then you couldn't touch me for nursery skills.)

Then, at the age of nine, I was recuperating at home following the removal of my tonsils. I'm not sure how it came to be, but I clearly remember a green costume laid out on my bed. Tights. Tunic. Cap with feather. That's right, I was Peter Pan. For two weeks, I wore nothing else, flying from bedroom window to the pirate's lagoon in the never-never land of my mind. I thank my lucky stars I had creative parents who would never shame a prepubescent boy into thinking that dolls and tights were somehow unseemly for a young male.

This was the fairy dust of childhood, and I sprinkled it with abandon.

During these early years, as the twin spells of theater and poetry worked their magic in me, my grandmother brought me to the Alpinelike village of Stowe. This was a thirty-minute ride from Burlington, Vermont, and, for a child, a trip to wonder. There we visited the Trapp Family Lodge, the adopted home of a family that had fled the Nazis in Austria, gaining renown as the subjects of the acclaimed musical *The Sound of Music* by Rodgers and Hammerstein.

The family would gather on the lawn in front of the lodge and, if you were lucky, perform a few songs. It was quite miraculous and entertaining for a child who loved music and theater in equal measure. The eldest of this family was a white-haired woman with ruddy checks. Looking nothing like Julie Andrews, this, indeed, was Maria, once governess and now mother figure to the rambling brood.

I remember meeting her and having her take my hand. I remember her voice, her music. We had the opportunity to walk amid the beautiful birches opposite her home. On several occasions as I was growing up I visited Maria, especially when I was old enough to drive myself. Even today I always go straight to that same grove of birch trees, the trees where

Maria had strolled, sharing the majesty of musical notes with a young boy. I would sing along with her then and was captivated by her dazzlingly blue eyes, which seemed to dance with her passion.

During one such visit, I remember singing to her a song she had once sung to me, looking eagerly at her for her approval. She smiled but shook her head slowly. Had I made a mistake? Had I sung the wrong notes?

"No," she said. "The notes are the right notes, but the song . . . the song is mine. Do you know what it is you must now do as you grow into a young man?" I hadn't a clue. She nodded, grinned, and opened her arms as if to embrace all of tomorrow. "You must find your own song. You must find Jan's song. And when you find it, you must sing it with your whole life."

At the time I wasn't aware of the simple and profound gift Maria gave me. But now, having climbed a fair portion of my life's mountains, I have found the truth of it resonates in me like a beloved instrument tenderly played. One of life's great quests, one that we are on even when we don't know it, is to find our own song and share it with the world.

Maria died some years later. I was, by then, a young adult, and I drove down to visit her grave at the foot of the mountains. Without thinking, I found myself wandering over to that circle of birches that I had visited so many times. I wept quietly and openly. But then a cool October wind braced me with its vitality, and something grew within me. Something that had taken root now shot out like a flowering branch rising up through me to touch the heavens.

I began to sing.

It was a simple song. A song of thanksgiving. A song for Maria, for the mountains, for the birch trees.

A song that seemed to celebrate my life, my hopes, my sense of being me.

I sang, I think, for the wonder of knowing people like my mom and dad and Maria, all of whom had taught me to breathe deeply the wonder in life. All of whom sang their own song. Walt Whitman called it a *Song of Myself.* I sang for that gift I now recognized in my own heart.

And the song has been mine ever since.

~

When we sing our own ideas, our own passions, when we share our own fears, give utterance to our own dreams, we are listening to the voice of our authentic selves. When we share it with the world, we produce the meaning that is only ours to share. Think to yourself how the world would be the poorer without our individual voices.

So take a moment to listen for your song today. And when you hear it, sing it. I don't care what kind of voice you have, it's the spirit of the sound you make. When you celebrate you, the truth of you, in word and deed and, yes, song, you kindle a bit more light.

Childhood was like that.

Adulthood can be, too.

Looking for Answers

Have you noticed that at the most challenging moments of your life, you find yourself seeking a higher power? It might be when you or someone you love is sick and, rusty though you may be, you're spinning prayers by the dozen. Or you fall in love, and you want the object of your affection to feel just the same way. You fire off a 9-1-1 to the divine: "If you *really* want me to believe in you, you'll make this happen." Or you're on a particularly bumpy plane ride, flying right through a monstrous storm, lurching from side to side, and suddenly you are cutting deals with the universe like there was no tomorrow.

Which brings me to a little piece of advice about good news and bad news.

It came to me from one of my dad's buddies when I was a high-school student back in Vermont. I had been rushing through the snow to my father's diner when I ran into Barney along Church Street, the main thoroughfare where half the town was on foot at any given moment. Barney's son had just won an academic award that morning at a school assembly, and, to my chagrin, I spilled the beans about it. As the words left my mouth, I was already kicking myself for not letting Barney hear the news from his own kid. I must have said as much out loud, but Barney smiled, a twinkle in his eye, comforting me. "Good news you tell right away," he assured me. "Bad news will always arrive soon enough."

I thought about that one afternoon, some thirty-one years later, when, just as Barney said it would, the bad news arrived soon enough.

We were losing Bonnie's pregnancy. Chromosomal damage. Chromosome number twelve.

Life has a way of mixing and matching, and every once in a while it gets it wrong. A prenatal procedure can point to an aberration of chromosomal makeup that allows doctors to guarantee with what amounts to a statistical certainty that your baby-to-be is damaged goods.

Nature will take its course, but it does not take into account the emotions of the parents. My wife, Bonnie, and I were left with an empty pang of what might have been.

There were tears and thoughts of "Why me?" and "Why us?" I found myself asking, Who put this sperm and this egg into orbit together? Didn't the ordered cosmos know that an extra piece of chromosome had attached itself in the process? I wanted to ask the universe to speak to me, explain it to me.

And while I was at it, I'd want to know about emphysema, the kind that killed my dad. I'd dig for some semblance of reason as to why a twenty-nine-year-old woman I worked with had to die of some aberration called ovarian cancer or why babies had to be afflicted with Down's syndrome or what good could come from HIV or . . . or any number of things.

I'd want answers. And I'd be prepared to listen as long as it took.

I've discovered, however, a simple truth. Sometimes the universe does not respond according to our timetable. And silence may also be a kind of answer—sometimes the only one we get. Furthermore, while the universe may wish to take its own time in getting back to us in a manner we can understand, life continues its forward motion. We forget sometimes that when we allow ourselves to be mired in obstinate demands for satisfaction, life can pass us by.

If we will but listen to life's rhythmic beat, we will recognize that getting on with life is, at times, the only answer that makes sense. And while we cannot control life's challenges, we hold the power to respond, and begin anew.

Maybe that was what I was listening for all along.

~

Even in difficult times, perhaps especially in difficult times, it could prove worthwhile to remember:

If we only listen for the answers we want we may miss the answers we need.

Mixed Messages

A little sign often appears at the bottom of restaurant menus and store entrances, and it has always struck me as a bit disconcerting:

We reserve the right to refuse service to anyone.

I get this mental picture of the owners standing behind some kind of one-way glass window, sizing us up as we enter. "Yeah, we can take her, he's all right, that family looks fairly normal. Wait a minute, I don't like the way that one's squinting—out!"

Don't misunderstand; I see the need to keep undesirables in check when you're running an enterprise. My dad owned a restaurant, and there was the occasional unsavory element that was a tad too rowdy or gave those waiting on them a hard time. You've got to protect yourself. It's just that I would like it to be done without anyone pointing it out to me. I'm aware that the little sign is there for legal reasons. Apparently you have to say it up front so no one misconstrues that they have the right to act in a way best suited for the World Wrestling Federation. It's just the juxtaposition of being welcomed into a business and being immediately put on notice that you could be asked to leave at any moment that strikes a discordant note. And, while I'm at it, if "the customer's always right," how can you actually refuse to serve her anything?

I think about the mixed messages we sometimes encounter in the business arena. This gets me thinking about the mixed messages we sometimes experience in the human arena.

Take the dating world, for instance. Going to meet someone on a date, wherever you fall on life's timeline, is all about wanting to make a connection. I mean, you don't go to all that bother because you want to dislike the person you're meeting. But if that's so, why do some people behave so obnoxiously that they are practically screaming to the unsuspecting date, "Go on—like me, I dare you"? I know a guy who purposely allows for lulls in the conversation just to see what the other person's really made of. I know a woman whose modus operandi with dates is to insist, somewhere at the top of the evening, that she has to leave early, just to find out if her date wants to be with her so badly the person will do anything to talk her out of it. These people misconstrue relationships as gamesmanship. You know the type?

Then there are the mixed messages we get when a friend or family member insists on doing anything to help us out and then is consistently busy every time we ask. Or the colleague who dismisses our ideas then appropriates them as his or her own. Or the person of authority who upholds the need for authority while abusing it.

Come to think of it, the messages aren't all so mixed after

all. Not if we listen to the complete communication. For the act of listening is performed, not only with our ears, but with our hearts. We "hear" with our feelings and discern the larger message—the attitude of one playing games with us, the desperation of another's aloofness. We become aware that these people are operating at a level not worthy of our time or attention. Our lives don't need that kind of disingenuousness, do they?

Of course not. But then why do we sometimes send mixed messages to ourselves? I'm talking about the times we tell ourselves we are absolutely, positively going to lose the weight beginning now while continuing to enjoy the customary sweets and late-night snacks that put it on to begin with. Or when we claim to ourselves that we want someone better in our lives, that we know we're worth it, while continuing to endure relationships that are destructive to our souls. Or the dreams we feed our hearts about following our passion, doing something of meaning in our lives, while never acting to extricate ourselves from work we find empty or, worse, demeaning.

If we really want to, we can walk away from those who give us mixed messages. We can decline a second date, figure out who we can truly count on, protect our ideas from an unethical colleague, and look to an authority who earns our trust. What we can't do is walk away from ourselves. When we're the generators of our own mixed messages, the only option, if we truly want to live a life that is everything we want it to be, is to listen to everything our life is saying.

Our souls must be allowed a voice. Our hearts must be allowed to speak. Our dreams must be allowed to name their desire. Listening to our souls, our hearts, our dreams, and the message in our actions all together is essential. If there is a cacophony of sound, one voice at odds with another, then we can do something about the discord. But only if we listen to the whole message, not simply the parts.

Listening to what our lives are saying brings an awareness of not only the mixed messages but also the meaningful ones. Listening to that kind of communication awakens within us a determination to let our lives speak with one voice, genuine and with purpose.

~

Of course, we can reserve the right to refuse service to ourselves. But it won't get us very far.

Authentic Voices

When I was a kid, Mike Corey was a hero. He owned the gas station next to my dad's diner, and he was a one-stop shop for all things automotive. No matter what went wrong with my father's Oldsmobile or my mom's old Pontiac, Mike miraculously knew just what was needed. I didn't think one man could know so much about any subject.

Hanging around the garage while waiting for my father to finish up at the restaurant, I'd watch Mike, all grease-covered arms and oil-stained clothes, squinting up at a car's underbelly as it sat atop the rack. He was an automotive detective pulling the universe apart then putting it back together better than before. He was an engine-healing, spark plug-fixing marvel, and somehow my life seemed a bit safer with Mike Corey around.

By the time I hit sixteen and attained the Holy Grail of a license, it was second nature that a ping or a leak or a kink in the ignition meant making a beeline for Mike's place. I didn't even have to steer; the car knew where to go. If you've ever had to deal with car repair—and who hasn't?—you know what I mean when I say that an old-fashioned all-purpose mechanic you can trust, the way we trusted Mike, is worth his weight in gold.

Which leads me to what passes for service stations in our current can't-catch-our-breath existence. Most of these automated fuel ports lack even a semblance of human contact. Some sequestered cashier hidden in a Plexiglas booth slides a robotic drawer in your direction, into which you dutifully place your cash or credit card. The whole transaction smacks of turning over your valuables in the county jail.

You got a ping? Fuggedaboudit.

Engine trouble? You kidding?

The anonymous character sheathed in the shack's got all she can do to put your money on the right pump. It's like placing a bet at the track: "Ten bucks on number five."

I keep waiting for the person behind the glass window to ask, "Is that to win, place, or show?"

ATMs? Same story. You get your money fast, but you don't get the minimum daily requirement of conversation. In this get-it-to-me-quick-or-don't-bother, card-swiping, code-punching, Internet-shopping world, taking a moment to actually converse with a real person is growing rare. Establishing a relationship with someone who actually knows something about her service area is rarer still.

We can do something about that.

Not all the Mike Coreys of the world have gone the way of the dodo bird.

You'll find him in a small-town diner where the owner is

the man actually cooking the food, serving up the pie he baked himself that morning.

You'll uncover him in the person of the tailor in the little local cleaner around the corner from the mammoth take-a-number version the whole city seems to use. He's the one who lets out the pants you'd had pressed on account of the few extra pounds he's noticed you're carrying since the holidays. Says he'll be happy to take them in when your New Year's resolution to lose weight kicks in.

She's the doctor who's actually willing to close the door for a heart-to-heart, who knows the names of your kids and has more than a fleeting connection to not only your body but your spirit as well.

The diner may not be flashy, the cleaner a few steps farther, the doctor in tighter quarters than those of some mighty HMO. Point is, they're out there, these wondrous people like Mike Corey who care about what they do. And perhaps of greater consequence to our spiritual health, they share their passion and authenticity with the rest of us. They're little miracles of the genuine article in an increasingly franchised world, worth the extra few paces or looking past the time-worn exterior.

Don't get me wrong. I use ATMs all the time. There's something to be said for no-nonsense transactions, especially when you're the one who's got to pick up dinner. Still, for the sake of expedience and to the glory of progress, I can't help but feel the human voice is growing a bit fainter.

We deserve better, don't we?

When we take the time to listen to those with whom we interact, be it a businessperson in a commercial transaction or the crossing guard at school, we can discover the authentic voices that remind us how strong, how passionate our own voice can be. When we listen to those who take pride in their work, who go about their business with genuine enthusiasm, who show an interest in others, we are reminded of how good life can be. For in such encounters we are listening to passion and caring personified.

Such awareness heightens our soul's humanity. Authenticity is part of what the universe is sending us if we'll tune our ears to the real thing.

~

Every once in a while, when I'm pumping my own gas at some sleek get-it-and-go establishment, in a hurry to get who knows where, I catch a voice from my past whispering in my ear.

"Hear that ping, kid? I can fix that for you."

I hear you, Mike. I hear you.

Touched by the Baton

In the small town of Lenox, tucked away in the Berkshires of Massachusetts, is a heavenly oasis on earth dedicated to celebrating music in all its permutations.

The Boston Symphony Orchestra makes its home there every summer. Native son James Taylor plays an annual concert. Dawn Upshaw's voice vibrates across the stage and out into the trees. John Williams conducts the Boston Pops. Nancy Wilson crowns the summer with jazz. Students study. Vocalizers vocalize. Composers compose. And it all bears the pedigree of Koussevitsky, Copeland, and Bernstein—artists who have been integral to its success.

On a summer's eve you'll find families, couples, and solitary souls spread across the lawn, under a tree or on a hilltop, picnicking, imbibing, awaiting that night's offering. When the evening's revelers first arrive, the sun is just starting its melt into sunset. Magical echoes of end-of-day rehearsals float from all corners of the enchanted property, and the instruments and voices play out in harmony with nature's symphony. Listening to this myriad of melodious sounds, you become suddenly permeated with the overwhelming awareness that we are, all of us, *very* lucky to be alive.

Tanglewood is touched by the baton of life's composer. The

stars that emerge in the postsunset sky shine upon the night's celebrants. As the music wafts out across the lawn, weaving its spell through trees, blades of grass, and human hearts, a peace steals across the grassy slope that is all the more precious for being so elusive in daily life.

But that is a problem often of our own making. And we, like all of creation, are capable of evolving. Instruction can be found in the glorious sounds and rhythms. As we listen, we are transported. No matter where music is celebrated, we can be touched by its magic, its ability to lift our spirits.

Setting aside any time can make a difference in your day: perhaps some work break hip-hop or a musical meditation at dawn, a symphony while fixing dinner, jazz at lunch, or, if you're musically inclined, a half hour or so noodling on the guitar, piano, or harmonica. Experiencing music daily helps to tune our psychic timpani.

We're all instruments in the orchestra of life, but without care our inner strings go flat. We lose the ability to make a joyful noise. As the artists of our own lives, we're responsible for our own tuning. And in order to properly tune, as any musician can tell you, we must first listen. If music shares a piece of heaven with the rest of us on earth, the least we can do is make the most of it.

Places like Tanglewood remind us that music *is* life, in all its notes, timing, moods, and harmonies.

You know, it would have been nice to share a picnic with Bernstein.

The Waters of Possibility

Marion gets up early each morning, racing the dawn to the day's promise. More often than not she swims a number of laps at the local sports club and is ready for work while most of us are still stirring in bed, contemplating the day's first transfusion of java.

I should pause to revisit this reference to Marion's aquatic exercise. The woman doesn't merely swim her laps. That would be way too conventional. No, what Marion does is this: fitting herself with a snorkel-like contraption that allows her to remain below the surface for long periods of time, she uses the underwater experience to prepare her workday agenda. While submerged—rubber domed, mouthpiece linking her to oxygen above the surface, her arms and legs a perpetual whirlwind—Marion is reviewing in her mind any number of tasks for the days or weeks ahead. Book proposals, clients to see, seminars to plan, a myriad of concerns, each to be contemplated and mentally filed.

The kicker here is that this vibrant woman, who makes sixty-five look like a splash in the fountain of youth, approaches each task with the anticipation of a child marveling at a mountain of birthday presents.

It occurs to me as I write these words that Marion lives the same way she swims—totally immersed. Each day she dips in the waters of possibility.

Marion is infused with the belief that life presents us with daily opportunities, and she doesn't intend to miss even one. Followed for a week or two, this recipe for living might serve to jump-start each of us out of passivity and into the realm of affirmation. Taken as a lifetime credo, this positive approach to each day is a veritable manifesto for meaning.

Marion grew up in a household where her brother was encouraged to excel, to seek out new trails and career directions. She, on the other hand, was in effect discouraged from dreaming. The pep talks and speculation on how far a kid could go centered solely on the boy of the family. With no role model to encourage her to spread her wings, she had to do what many women of generations ago had to do if they were to fly as high as their dreams: she broke the mold.

Relying on her own self-determination, her own innate wisdom, Marion created a tomorrow that no one else would help her imagine. With gritty reliance on her own abilities, she made her way through school, found a husband who would be a partner in building up, not tearing down, and she soared. Years later, with husband Matt cheering her on as her parents never had, Marion got that Ph.D., becoming a renowned and well-respected clinical psychologist.

Marion is a woman who engages you easily in conversation.

When I first met her, the warmth was barely off her handshake before we were involved in a serious and challenging conversation about the meaning of existence. While she openly points out the hypocrisies she sees in organized religion, I have come to find her remarkably spiritual—in fact, deeply so.

Her spiritual wealth springs from her constant sense of wonder, her gratefulness for the experience of being alive. It's embodied in her sense of living in the moment, in the day, in her physical engagement of the elements and her passionate exchange of ideas. Marion's is a kind of upturned awe as she jumps heart-first into the world.

Such gratefulness lived fully touches powerfully upon the soul. It evokes an eternal *yes!* It is that *yes* to which I aspire. To find opportunity in each new day. To welcome that opportunity like I have a right to it. To recognize that there is a contribution that only I can make. Such is the power of her example.

Each of us, if we pay attention, can find these mentors in our midst, people who show and tell us how good life can be. When we hear the voice of someone worth listening to, we know it, for it's a voice that resonates in that place within us where truth and what Buddhists call "right mindfulness" reside.

So I listen to Marion when she speaks. I listen for the infectious passion, the bounty of original thought, the authenticity of her exuberance and reflection. I listen for the richness of her life's song.

~

You see, I've learned this little secret about life from my mother-in-law, Marion:

Your glass can never be empty when you drink from the waters of possibility.

soundtrack

I don't know about you, but at times the daily American soundtrack, with its squabbling political junkies, talk radio vigilantes, and testimonials to shattered lives, is enough to sink my soul.

It's not that fear of bioterrorism, recession, or sexual impotence are not fascinating subjects or what star is divorcing what other star is not intensely germane to my personal future and that of my fellow citizens. I mean, there's got to be something there, right? The cross-generational women of *The View* must know what's on America's mind. Why, Larry King fronts some of these stories, and he's on CNN. Plus he wears suspenders. On camera! You gotta trust a fella like that. It's simply that I'm not sure we need to hear it over and over and over, talk show tirade after radio rant, as if pandering to obsession with pain were some kind of virtue.

Don't misread me. I'm not advocating we give up publicly discussing these social issues. It's just that it seems to me there are only so many ways you can promote stories of fear and rejection before you become part of the problem.

Which leads me to the Dalai Lama.

Several years ago, at the Tibetan leader's request, a group of Jewish leaders gathered to share the story of their people.

The exiled holy man was interested in finding out how the Jews, through hundreds of years of wandering, had managed to survive and remain creative. It was his fervent hope to share these strategies with his own oppressed community, cut off from the lifeline of their historic home. Rodger Kamenetz movingly tells the story of this historic interchange in his book *The Jew in the Lotus*.

One day, in a private audience with the Dalai Lama, one of the rabbis was asked to share the story of the Shoah, the Holocaust. He gently demurred. Surely this great Buddhist leader, well read and traveled, had heard more than his share of accounts about the Nazi horror. Why would he want to be put through one more? The revered leader kindly pressed on.

"But I wish to hear *your* story," he said.

A gift of wisdom is found in that simple request. Each of us has our own particular story in life that is worthy of being told. Sometimes others create a space for us to do so, and then it is up to us to step into that loving opening and be heard.

So the rabbi began, recalling personal details of his own family's tragic fate at the hands of Hitler.

After a few minutes the rabbi noticed that tears were falling from the eyes of his listener. Oh, my, he thought, moved and a bit unsettled at the sight, I'm actually making the Dalai Lama cry. But carry on he did, weaving his tale of sadness and sacrifice with great energy.

The rabbi was wound up now, caught in the drama of his own words, when suddenly he felt a hand gently pressing on his shoulder. He looked up to face the holy man.

"But I'm not finished," he softly protested, noticing the Dalai Lama's eyes filled to overflowing.

"I know," replied His Holiness. "And I want to listen to it all. But . . . I need to hear something else now."

And in that response lay another world of wisdom. He acknowledged simply that we need to balance not only what we take into our bodies but also what we take into our hearts.

If we ingest a steady diet of sensationalism or sadness or even boycott it with mindless unbridled levity, we remain in an unbalanced state, unaware of our very lack of equilibrium. Which is why we need to listen to our own lives. We need to listen for our soul's needs and our heart's requirements. We can alter the daily soundtrack of our lives and, in so doing, achieve a stability that may be missing. Balance in what we hear leads to balance in what we say, what we experience, what we do. In other words, we need to feed our soul's yin as well as yang.

~

If we listen to the soundtrack of our lives, we can achieve not only the good life we seek but, even more soul nourishing, a life of *goodness*.

True Beauty

Beauty possesses the amazing grace of inhabiting this earth in places and persons we might least suspect. And finding beauty in such unexpected locales transcends wonder; it affirms life.

In a world where physical attributes take on the status of icons, where the outer appearance of a setting or individual is often the only measure of worth, we do well to reclaim an essential truth—the ultimate beauty is that of the soul. And such beauty grows from the inside out.

The last place I would expect to find such splendor is in South Central Los Angeles—home of gangs, guns, and graffiti. I had heard from several people who knew my penchant for finding people of passion that in South Central could be found an amazing woman who had created a remarkable institution, A Place Called Home. Traveling into gang territory was not my idea of a cultural outing, but if that was where the woman of wonder was making things happen, I wanted to see it with my own eyes.

As I drove down Central Avenue, some ten minutes from Los Angeles' City Hall, I was confronted with a rough-looking, graffiti-covered street of businesses and bodegas, an American thoroughfare that had clearly not known the benefit of fresh paint or neighborhood beautification for some time.

Turning the corner, I arrived at my destination. Behind barbed wire and chain-link fencing sat a clean, cared-for large building housing A Place Called Home. Not a letter of graffiti was on it.

Inside I met a woman who had come through the wringer of life and come out empowered, creative, and vibrant. Debrah Constance is five feet, three inches of human dynamite—hope personified. Having fought the battles of alcoholism, physical abuse, and cancer, she has taken her pain and crystallized it into possibility. Here in the midst of violence and despair she has chosen to build a place where children can come after school for a kind word, a snack, help with schoolwork, a chance to sample the arts.

It all came about after a friend confronted her at a most vulnerable moment in her recovery and asked a simple and profound question: "What do you really want to do with your life?"

Debrah listened to that question. More important, in listening to it, she allowed herself to hear in the question life's potential and her own actualization. She decided to use what savings she had to set up a storefront in an area where children would most need to feel safe. She also wanted to make a statement, consciously or not: that all children have the right to a caring and nurturing atmosphere and to a tomorrow where they can drive their dreams as far as their hearts will go.

Debrah showed me a room where dance classes are taught by accomplished choreographers; she showed me a space for art, a workout facility, and a music studio. She proudly escorted me to a school annex, where teenagers who may not make it in the public setting get another chance to complete their studies and move ahead. Hundreds and hundreds of children attend classes or after-school programs. All because a woman listened to a question. All because a woman listened to the *yes* that existed in her own heart.

I have gone back many times to visit and take part in the life-force pulsing in South Central. Speaking to Debrah or her associate, Sister Pat, a Roman Catholic nun who is serving the community through her work at A Place Called Home, I realize I am listening to true beauty personified. I hear the thrill they feel as they listen to the excitement and creative wonder emerging from children who know that love means an arm around the shoulder, a word of caution when counsel is necessary, a warm snack before homework, someone who is willing to listen to your dreams.

Take a moment today to listen to your heart. Hear the dreams that are percolating, waiting to burst out. Listen to the question asked of Debrah—*What do you really want to do with your life?* Our answers may change over time, but now, in this moment, we can realize that the true beauty of our lives can be obscured only by our own indifference. The will to act is all that is missing to make real the power of our dreams.

Meeting Debrah was an affirmation of life. It helped destroy my stereotypes of where and when beauty can be found. A miracle of the human spirit is taking place in South Central Los Angeles. Former gang members have come to believe there is a future beyond bullets and boundaries.

~

Listening to your heart can lead to promises fulfilled.

Life can be *this* good when we give our dreams the wings to fly.

Rules from the Tavern of Life

According to tradition, in 1773, one Samuel Pepoon established a small tavern on the main street corner of Stockbridge, Massachusetts. Over the entrance he placed the image of a regal lion, a tip of the hat to the British who still controlled the colonies. Passengers of the horse-drawn coaches traversing the dusty roads between Albany and Boston would stop at Sam's place for a cool draft to quench their thirst. In July of the following year, an angry citizenry gathered at the tavern to pass resolutions, protesting England's repressive acts of intolerance. It was in Pepoon's courtyard where they determined to boycott British goods, raising the defiant flag of liberty and, no doubt, a few pints of Pepoon's finest.

Since those days, the Red Lion Tavern evolved into the Red Lion Inn and has hosted an eclectic mix of notables, among them Teddy Roosevelt, Eleanor Roosevelt, Henry Wadsworth Longfellow, and a defiant young folksinger, Bob Dylan.

The times may have always been a changin', but the magnificent Red Lion has kept faith with this corner of America. History abounds from its rambling white porch overlooking the bustle of Main Street in this quintessential New England village. Today's tavern, located in the rear of the inn, bears the ambiance, if not the actual timber, of its pre-Revolutionary origins.

On the side door of the tavern opening out into Sam Pepoon's old courtyard, you'll find a fascinating list of regulations known as the "Rules of the Tavern." I spent some time musing on their colorful contents, which are as follows:

> Four pence a night for bed.
> Six pence with potluck.
> Two pence for horse keeping.
> No more than five to sleep in one bed.
> No boots to be worn in bed.
> No razor grinders or tinkers taken in.
> No dogs allowed in the kitchen.
> Organ grinders to sleep in the washhouse.
> Signed, Lemuel Coxs, innkeeper.

That's a lot of *no*'s to heed.

Now we no longer use pence in our monetary system, and I've never met a razor grinder in my wanderings. I'm not even sure I want to know what an organ grinder did that would land him in the washhouse. But the very existence of these colorful regulations gets me thinking about the kind we might tack up at the entrance to our own life's tavern. Only I'd like our contemporary rules to be filled with affirmation of what we can do, ought to do, to make life as good as we want it to be. That means listening to more *yes*es, more about allowing possibility *in* than about keeping experiences and people *out*.

The rules I'm contemplating are for our soul's ears. They're for listening to with hearts that can hear the hope in a single day. The sort of rules that remind us that through paying attention to small and natural gifts, like the power of touch and the magical lift of a kind word, we're able to drink ever more fully from life's heady brew.

~

The following, inspired by the innkeeper, are my rules for the tavern of life:

> Three hugs to start your day.
>
> Multiple kisses on any child's boo-boo.
>
> The same for adults.
>
> Time to be set aside daily for music or meditation.
>
> Five minutes of gazing at a full moon each time it appears.
>
> Encouragement to be spoken to others weekly.
>
> The same to your own heart.
>
> Two full quaffs from the wonder of life every twenty-four hours.
>
> Moments set aside to listen to the positive in each new day.

Oh, yes . . .

And everyone's allowed in the kitchen.
Always.
Dogs included.

Open...

When one door closes another opens; but we often look so regretfully upon the closed door that we do not see the one which opens for us.

ALEXANDER GRAHAM BELL

Life Can Be *This* Good
When We Open

The ability to listen, and to hear the sacred sparks of life in the midst of an ordinary day, leads us to our next step in gaining access to the riches that are ours for the taking—opening a place within our hearts to make room for these gifts. As we listen for the sounds of affirmation around us, we open ourselves to increased understanding and awareness.

This unlocking of our spirit is no less than a gift of wings. We were meant to soar, you and I. It is our destiny to discover the wonder in the human and the humanity in the wonder.

So often, we become filled up with the mundane: bills, work demands, the static emotional circle of "shoulda-woulda-coulda." By clearing that out, widening our inner spaces, we open ourselves to the potential for daily renewal.

Suddenly, the gentle touch of a loved one's hand, the sweetness of a friend who cares, our own innate passion—all have room in our lives and are revealed for the life affirmations they are.

To *listen* is to attune ourselves to how good life can be. Being *open* allows that good to flow in.

As we open our hearts to the wealth found in our daily experiences, we learn of the potential within us. It is in living with passion and purpose, discarding the false and laying claim to the human, that we open within us the personal power of our own possibilities.

Allow the wonder of creation to blow freely through you. Kiss the day by welcoming it into the space you have created. The blessing is in that opening.

And in the meaning that fills that place you have opened, you will hear the universe confirm: *you* are a blessing.

Indiana Jones comes to Nantucket

The simplest surprises are dropped into our lives in moments of serendipity, and the soul gets a whole new song to sing.

It was the summer of 1996, and I was licking my wounds from the life-shattering experience that comes with ending a relationship. On a journey of healing, I took to the road of my native Northeast, searching for I knew not what. Sometimes answers are there when we want them; other times just asking the questions can be answer enough.

It was my Thoreau summer, and the whole of New England was my Walden Pond. I drove the back roads of my home state of Vermont, listening to a soundtrack of Tracy Chapman, James Taylor, Carly Simon, and John Coltrane. I gloried in the beauty of the small towns and villages of Massachusetts and New Hampshire as if discovering them for the first time. I was in need of the familiar, the touchable world where I could once again be grounded. Which makes me slightly amused to tell you that my next stop was a ferry traveling from Cape Cod to an island thirty miles out to sea.

Nantucket—a place that conjures long summer days and sand dunes unfolding with the grace of tradition and native Yankee gusto. As soon as I'd settled into my bed-and-breakfast, I got hold of a bike and hit the paths that crisscrossed the island. En route to the town of Sconset, and feeling a familiar hunger, I detoured off the trail to the local airport. Arriving at a quaint gray clapboard building, I nosed around a bit, wolfed a doughnut and a cup of coffee, and headed back out for a glorious ride.

I had just begun to cycle away when the face of a stranger sitting on the lone wooden bench along the curb came into view. A smile of recognition washed over me. I paused, straddling my bike a few feet away, wondering if I should say something. I was never one to disturb the famous. Nevertheless, seeing the composer before me, alone and vulnerable, I felt my reserve crumbling. (It didn't occur to me at the time that I was the one who was alone and vulnerable and this was all a projection.)

So I spoke up in the most noninvasive, nonfanlike, unadoring manner I could muster:

"This is incredible. You're John Williams! I mean, you're John Williams?"

Williams grinned, and I swear his eyes twinkled. What he didn't do was lower his head, retreat, mumble hello, or try to brush me off—responses to which, in hindsight, he was clearly entitled.

"I am here to conduct a summer concert," he said by way of explaining his presence. "Waiting for my ride."

Taking his conversational response as the smallest of openings, I leaned over my handlebars to deliver a message to which only the two of us were privy: "Your music . . . has meant something to me."

The minute those words left my lips, I felt myself transformed into a walking, talking, cycling cliché. How many times must this Academy Award-winning composer have heard that? Yet he drew me in.

"Come, sit down a moment," he replied, motioning me to the bench beside him. "Tell me, which piece do you like best?"

The man seemed genuinely interested. This I couldn't believe. But sit I did, telling him with great animation of my admiration for *E.T.,* the score of *Schindler's List,* the bravado of *Star Wars*—all comments he must have heard a million times but listened to as if for the first.

"But *Indiana Jones,*" I concluded, "for some reason, wherever and whenever I hear it, always fills me with a sense of adventure. The blood starts pumping, and, I don't know, maybe it's silly, but it always makes me feel just a bit—"

I stopped myself. It would sound too corny. But his eyes held mine as if to reassure me that nothing I could say would be corny to him and my confession was safe. I put my head down a moment then lifted it back up to face him. "Heroic."

Immediately I kicked myself. So, Goldstein, you feel heroic? Who the hell cares? Leave that to Harrison Ford, for pity's sake.

But Williams didn't blanch. He held me in the embrace of those twinkling eyes, the gentle warmth of his attention, and the passionate interest in a stranger's opinion of his work. "Good," he said. "That was my idea in composing it. I'd hoped you'd feel that way."

He was genuinely delighted, and I was touched beyond expression. This man, a paradigm of creativity, was, after all, a human being. Like you and me, he appreciated being appreciated. By allowing an opening for our connection, he allowed a gift to take root between us. He had not become jaded, and my stopping on that summer's day seemed to make a difference. In fact, more than a difference—it was meaningful. It mattered.

After promising to catch his concert on the beach the next night, I thanked him for the chat and hopped up on my bike. With a wave I was on my way. Rounding a corner, I headed alongside the fence of the airfield, a lift taking hold of me.

~

In my summer of healing and renewal, this brief interchange had been both revelation and affirmation. *The simplest surprises are dropped into our lives in moments of serendipity, and the soul gets a whole new song to sing.* In being open to me, Williams had helped create an opening *within* me, one in which the song of renewal could exist.

As I cycled alongside the fence of the airfield, humming a theme, I was Indiana Jones riding out on a new adventure. And at just that moment, music in my heart, soul riding high, taking in the series of small aircraft parked at the edge of the airfield, it occurred to me: the planes here were grounded.

It was I who was flying.

The Menehune Are for Real

On the island of Kauai, the oldest of the Hawaiian Islands, they tell the legend of a group of little people who materialize only at night to perform seemingly impossible tasks. Known as the Menehune, these diminutive workers, it is said, were responsible for having built the remarkably massive dam that exists near the south center of Kauai. Fashioned out of red dirt, it is an amazing feat of watery architecture. As late as the mid-nineteenth century, the mythical Menehune were counted in a survey of the king's people.

Like Ireland's leprechauns, the little people of Kauai work their magic under the moonlight. The Menehune appear to be dreams floated on the consciousness of an island, borne on the currents of the night, where the mystical meets the imagination. They therefore take on a magical reality within the psyche of Kauai's native culture.

Our minds and hearts often combine to fashion new characters that come to populate our lives. Sometimes they take the form of creatures like Caliban, part man, part monster, who suffers his demons on Prospero's island in *The Tempest*. He is the embodiment of torment, his life producing only pain and evil thoughts, the products of long-held grudges that have twisted his soul.

Also on the isle we can find Ariel, a sprightly character who can perform magic to further the goals of her master. Seeking her own freedom, Ariel heeds the bidding of Prospero in his attempt to right ancient wrongs and garner a measure of redemption for himself and those he loves.

When we latch onto past grievances and breathe life into them, they take up space in our lives, tormenting us with old demons made new day after day by our inability or unwillingness to let them go. We come to welcome the Calibans of anguish as part and parcel of the world we know, a world where we keep our own lives from moving forward, twisting ourselves into unpleasing shapes of frustration and despair. A world that, sadly, has become oddly comfortable in its familiarity. It never occurs to us that since it is *we* who create and perpetuate this mythical creature in our own souls, we own the power to reshape it.

Each one of us can, if we will, fashion from the clay of our imaginations positive creations, Ariel-like, that further our goals of liberation from so limiting an isle of despair. What kind of liberation?

Freedom from the negative we've allowed to take up residence in our hearts.

Freedom from the torment of past grievances that burrow into the sinew of our souls.

Freedom from the shackles of distrust and distortion that

limit our ability to walk out into the warm light of hope.

Freedom from the skewered outlook that prevents our seeing the wonder of free choice.

Which creature will we give life to on the island of our daily lives?

We alone possess the ability to mold our demons into creatures of redemption, to open our hearts to the Menehune-like outlook that emanates beauty instead of ugliness. The people of Kauai choose to see nature's splendor as springing forth from the creativity of the little people. The Menehune, our creative selves, can be very real. We must simply open the doors within us that trap the debilitating attitudes and allow that space to be replaced by the power of our own possibilities.

Start by letting go of one grudge today. The Hawaiians say, "*E menehune mai kakou i ka hana,*" which translates as, "Let's get together and get the work done like Menehune." Forgive one person—a family member, a friend, yourself—for some past wrong. Dousing the fires of a past anger and granting forgiveness will open you to the wonder of your soul's liberation.

~

The creatures of liberation will come to life within us if we open the lines of communication between who we are and who we want to be. Not just today, but every day.

when Heaven and Earth Kiss

For my money, a good sunset is the cheapest shot of wonder out there. Think of it—bursts of incandescent energy that can curl your toes, warm your soul, and prove cost effective all at the same time. The iciest hearts on the planet can be thawed by the heaven's burnished flame. Countries sitting down for peace talks ought to begin with a joint viewing of rose-dipped hues and golden halos merging into growing flowers of light. And for romance, this daily dose of celestial seduction is just what the love doctor ordered.

I remember as a teenager getting the notion that girls liked being kissed at sunset. My teenage girlfriends were part of my research. I was sure no one else was on to it and that this part of my repertoire would single me out for glory. I couldn't miss. The way I figured, a sunset occurs when heaven and earth kiss. It was God's way of telling us to do the same.

I imagined every girl I kissed in this revolutionary manner would quite naturally spread the revelation. I was soon disappointed, though; my reputation failed to grow exponentially.

More recently, when first meeting the incredible woman who is now my wife, I quickly caught what Bonnie was about when I asked the age-worn question, "So, what do you do?"

"I chase sunsets," she replied.

I was a goner. I'm not sure if that was the exact moment I fell in love, but it was, at least, the start of my descent.

Cut to our honeymoon and one of my favorite settings in the world—Ireland, the Emerald Isle. One day we were traveling from the city of Galway, thrilling to the western coast of this beautiful and mist-shrouded country, toward the much-heralded Ring of Kerry. Late in the afternoon we discovered that a boat up ahead could ferry us across a tributary and save some four hours' driving time. I made for the last launch, a mere ten minutes and eighteen kilometers away. With luck, and no livestock crossings, we would just make it.

Passing through an eyesore of a town called Lahinch, I caught site of its pittance of a rocky beach. For a moment I thought of the home waiting for us back in California, ten minutes from Santa Monica and Malibu's smooth stretches of sand and ocean. Now *those* were beaches.

All of a sudden Bonnie called out, "Stop!"

Was she crazy? Had I heard right? Stop? We needed every precious second to make the ferry, or we'd end up staying in this godforsaken outpost. Stop? She couldn't possibly be serious!

She could, and she was.

Dutifully, I pulled over with an oceanic sigh that could drown a country full of honeymooners. What could be so important that we should miss the last boat? Bonnie pointed to the sky and smiled back at me with a glow I will never forget. It was the sunset. Not just any sunset. This clearly was a masterpiece.

Getting out, we started over to the rocks along the shoreline. Arm in arm, we drank deep of a heavenly show of amber and golden hues, rose finger clouds painting the broad canvas of sky.

It was a moment of incandescence—and had my bride not been a chaser of sunsets, someone who was open to nature's wonders, I would have missed it completely.

The bridge would wait another day. The Ring of Kerry wasn't going anywhere. Bonnie and I inhaled the magnificent sunset like ambrosia. At its apex, sitting in silence, she turned to me, giving me a kiss that glowed from the inside out.

Nothing I'd done as a teenager or as an adult had ever felt that full or complete.

Sunsets, and sunrises for that matter, are gifts served up in plentiful procession. It's one of life's ways of taking a simple pause, marking the day. If we're too busy, caught in the whirlwind of our own manufacturing, we miss the magic. What is required in order to drink the heady miracle of morning or evening light is a consciousness of *how* we use the time allotted us each day. We must be willing to open up room in our everyday schedules for what really pays dividends. This requires a simple and purposeful cessation of activity. Pausing for a moment, we willingly open our spirits to the gifts of the universe. These are indeed the gifts that help make life *this* good.

~

When we stop to open ourselves to the beauty of a sunset, we create an awareness of our own incandescence. We too burn with a shimmering flame.

As nature does, so we must mark time with a pause.

If for no other reason than it all goes by too darn fast.

when it comes to gambling, bet on your heart

As I write, two families in the Midwest have just won the lottery and will split something like $381,000,000. That's three hundred and eighty-one *million* dollars. I have a hard time wrapping comprehension around a sum that big. The insanity of it all boggles the mind.

Take a deep breath. Now imagine . . .

You toil all your life just to get by and one day you're driving home from a long shift and you stop for gas and as long as you're there you realize you're thirsty so you grab a soda and as you're paying for the gas and the soda, you take a few lottery tickets in change, tuck them into your back pocket and head home and the next night they pick the winner and lo and behold a couple of numbers sound familiar to you so you reach into the pocket and pull out the tickets and you are a multi-multimillionaire—all because of six numbers falling into place and the fact that you needed gas and a soft drink.

Whew.

Hey, this is America, home of Madonna and Oprah, where one can turn adversity and sheer will into stardom. Home of computer empires being forged in garages. Home of instant millionaires. And are we discouraged that only an infinitesimal teensy tiny few will ever hit the big one? Fuggedaboudit. It's the dream, folks. The wild pie-in-the-sky realization that it could be you as well as the next person. That's what keeps it all going.

Yet despite the white-hot excitement of winning a lottery, there are moments in our lives that make hitting the proverbial jackpot pale in comparison.

These are moments that touch the soul. And because they do, we don't just taste a fleeting morsel of heaven, we inhale life. These are the instances when our hearts are kissed by spirit and the breath of life is pumped into our being as if for the first time.

It might occur with the touch of a loved one recovering from illness.

The reunion of long-lost lovers.

The birth of a child or a grandchild.

That first pure kiss connecting you with your soulmate.

The final shared moment before someone close to you dies.

Or any number of sacred moments that your mind is recalling right now. This experience is plucked from a place in you money can't touch. It transcends lotteries, even hard-earned wealth, for it forms the apex of our humanity. These are the sacred moments of our lives, and we all have them at one time or another.

Every one of us.

Even-better-than-winning-the-lottery moments can be filled with the bittersweetness of loss and redemption. The one I'm going to share with you belongs to my sister, Ethel.

My sister was and is the only daughter born in a family of three other siblings, all boys. Born last, she was the apple of her daddy's eye. Named for my father's mother, Ethel Faith grew with the poetic perspective of our mother and the theatrical passion of our father.

In my family we all drink life with an enormous thirst, but my sister possesses a singular and striking earthiness and passion born of our Vermont roots. She is a vital human being, teeming with conviction and creativity, and the elementary children she teaches receive a gift beyond imagination just being in her presence and under her tutelage.

Throughout her life, her bond with our dad was truly heart touching and transformative. When Ethel experienced marital woes and the trials that came with divorce and single parenthood, my father felt the pain intensely and personally. And when he died, Ethel was inconsolable.

Several years went by before Ethel met a special man, one who loved her with a fortitude and loyalty that matched our dad's integrity. On the morning of her marriage to John, she put on her wedding dress, brimming with thanksgiving for the new life upon which she was about to embark. Taking in her reflection in the mirror, she was suddenly felled by intense sadness. As she sat down on the edge of her bed, a realization hit her, filling her with such a sense of lost opportunity that she felt her heart would break.

"Daddy," she called out in hushed tones, "I finally got it right . . . and you're not here." Her head bent back against her pillow, hair cascading down as it had when our father tucked her in as a little girl.

In the next instant, out of the darkness of her sorrow came light. And my sister, years later, tells of this moment with tears welling in her eyes. At that exact instant, the intense pain of our father's absence met her exquisite joy in her marriage to John.

"I'm right here, Ethel," came the warm whisper of our father's voice, and a million blessings flooded her soul.

I don't care how many million dollars you win, you'll never touch a moment like this with money. It comes only with the opening of your heart.

～

Recall one such gift when your breath was taken away by the sheer wonder of a redemptive voice, touch, or experience with nature. Cherish that memory by opening that space within you more often. Determine to be aware whenever it happens again. And it will.

That's no gamble; that's a sure bet.

unplanning a Day

Ever have one of those days when you're just not sure which foot to put out there first? You slowly come to consciousness, wipe the sleep from your eyes, and discover you have no firm idea about where the day's going to take you? Opening to a day like that is a little like giving yourself a party with an invitation list of one.

I recognize that a lot of us are planners. We line up our appointments, arrange for play dates for our kids, pencil in the plumber, and organize the smallest details of our lives. Some of us get so busy with all the plans and people and daily preparations that we actually have to schedule in our free time. (Scheduled free time—is that an oxymoron?)

Some of us plan our days with the use of little colored posting papers we stick up all over the house—on phones, refrigerators, or mirrors. Others use voice-mail, leaving ourselves all sorts of reminders—dates and appointments and matters that need our attention.

Of course, in this genre of planner is the subspecialty known as the list maker. Some people react as if they might lose their psychological footing if the game plan for the day isn't laid out there in black and white or highlighter. Some mentally compose the list the night before, while others keep it clipped to a day planner, a timeline lifeline for the memory challenged.

And there's nothing wrong with being prepared. Mapping out a blueprint for what needs to be accomplished can be a powerful tool for organization and success. It's just that running our lives by lists and day planners leaves little room for the unexpected and accidental, which can be serendipitous and surprising. Seems to me that every once in a while we need to put all the plans and the lists and the psychic blueprints aside and just let a day wash over us.

The thought actually scares some people. What do you mean, starting a day not knowing what I'm going to do? What kind of irresponsible act is that? But then, don't we owe a responsibility to the child within us? The harness of time we place around our daily activities needs to come off every once in a while, if only to allow our imagination and spirit the chance to roam more freely. Make sense?

Okay. So, here's my list for how this works.

- No lists.
- Accept no other offers that will occupy you that day.
- Upon awaking, allow the blank page of the day's canvas to serve as an invitation.
- Try taking breakfast or your cup of tea or coffee in a different setting—a garden, your bedroom, a café you've always wanted to try but never had time to visit. I have been known to sip a mug of cocoa on a rooftop, albeit a

very low roof, if for no other reason than to give myself a different perspective on familiar surroundings.

- Get in the car, and let it take you to a part of the city you've never visited or, when possible, down a country road. Or leave the car for a day and walk; just let your feet figure out which foot to put before the other. There are discoveries around many a corner that we can never see from the vantage point of a driver's seat or public transportation.

- Again, be aware of your mind's bent to start making plans while you're immersed in a day without a blueprint.

Now, of course, I've just made a list on how to spend a day free of them, which only goes to show that rules are made to be broken. Which is part of what we're doing in enjoying a day without plans—breaking the rules that govern our daily existence, opening new spaces for discoveries that can nourish the child inside us or provide new colors for our inner artist to use on our life's canvas.

Our unplanned day may take us inside a shop of antiques, where we'll meet an incandescent woman of a certain age who has the hippest views of how to live the good life.

Our unplanned day may lead us to a public garden we'd never noticed, where kids are growing a banquet of squash and snow peas and pumpkins as a school project for the local shelter.

Our unplanned day may unfold with silences that allow us to hear what we've been missing in the pressured heartbeat of a bottom-line world. Look—there's a neighbor we've never spoken to, a country path never explored, a book we've never opened and therefore never enjoyed.

Our day without lists may flow into a new appreciation for the energy we possess in the workplace and at home, an appreciation of our own merits that we often fail to consider. It may waft over us like the aroma of a home-cooked meal we've been too occupied to enjoy, picking up fast food and prepared meals as time-savers in our overplanned universe.

Our unplanned day may be anything it wants to be, even leading to the serendipitous making of a new friend or the surprise meeting of an old acquaintance whose path we never would have crossed had we not opened the gift of unplanned time.

Of course, the irony of finding a day without plans is that we probably have to plan for it. And it may prove a bit tougher if there are young children involved. Be creative.

Unplanning a day is one of the ways we show ourselves that life can be *this* good. It awakens the soul and opens the heart not only to the child within us but to the adult within who can still embrace that child.

~

So go on. Open up an unplanned day. Give yourself a turn every so often at the circus of life without any restrictions. Hold it in your heart.

Check it out. You're breathing deeper now.

And, for a brief interlude, the only note you make to yourself is the one that reminds you, *Do this again.*

The Miracle of Geoffrey

In an age of Harry Potter wizards and the unfulfilled dreams of the twenty-first century, Geoff Halpern was a miracle. There was about him a mystical quality, as if he carried some age-old secret embedded in his heart. In the midst of his painful life, filled with medical procedures to cleanse his blood, boost his trembling organs, and give him more time, Geoff managed to circumnavigate a lifetime in fifteen brief years.

From his earliest days, Geoff faced insurmountable odds. His was a life of hospital stays, doctor visits, leaving school early, or not showing up at all. When Geoff became a student of mine, as a young teen, he was living as if tethered to mortality. Every dawn brought the awesome challenge of persevering one more day. And while Geoff was climbing a multitude of medical mountains, his family was making the trek right alongside him with a gift of life and love that served as a guiding light on his difficult journey.

I remember a conversation I had with Geoff when he'd had a particularly rough time of it. He seemed ready to give up on existence. He hated hospitals, doctors, everything medical. And then we talked about his growing up. With a twinkle in his eye, he told me that when he got older he'd become a doctor. "But you detest doctors," I marveled. "Yes," he answered, with a firm display of confidence, "and I'll show them *how* you're supposed to treat sick children. I'll show them what a doctor *can* be."

Wow. That was Geoff, a walking affirmation in the midst of pain.

It's never easy to watch someone you care for suffer—to listen as they claw verbally at life. It was all his family could do just to keep hope alive, and yet this boy, this young man, with so much on his shoulders managed, to the bewilderment of the rest of us, to *smile.*

Yes, smile. That is the wonder of it all.

I experienced Geoffrey in full splendor, with jokes and bright eyes and challenges—a vital human being. There are people walking through life who don't begin to radiate the vitality Geoff did on his toughest day. This kid was not checking out. He ran for and won the office of president of his middle school. And he was more than a leader; he was an inspiration.

The best talks we shared were about God. Geoff hated God. He was at war with him. He had every right to protest; his condition demanded no less. How many days had he gone with classmates to the sports field and sat on the sidelines, not able to play? How often had he looked the other way when youngsters wolfed down a slice of pizza while he sipped his liquid staple out of a bottle? And still he found a way to be there, in the moment, embracing life.

In his last days in the hospital, Geoff and I talked of death. It was not an easy subject to broach, but Geoff, as always, appreciated honesty. He asked me what death was like. He asked if he would see his family again. We spun together the image of a garden of light where souls return to God after death. He thought he would find them there one day. He told me how much he was going to miss his mom, his dad, his sister. He told me that he wanted to hold on to life as long as possible but that he knew death was coming. And then, in a heartbreaking moment in which I brushed my hand across his forehead, certain I was witnessing a final grasp of life, he managed one more smile.

Small, almost imperceptible, but it was there all right. As if he *willed* that smile forward from his heart. This teenager's extraordinary capacity to look life in the face, challenge the pain, and then manage to produce a twinkle and a grin to light up the darkness was a true miracle.

For the rest of us, every day is another opportunity to embrace what and whom we love. We who are not in the grip of a fatal illness have the chance to create more life. It's ironic that this lesson to open, every day, to how precious life is comes to us by way of those who are dying.

I am convinced that many of the most vibrant seekers of

wonder are those who do not and cannot take life for granted—those with cancer, AIDS, MS, or a debilitating condition who see themselves, not as victims, but as survivors.

Since we have the example of loved ones as well as strangers whose challenging stories we come to know, as you now know Geoffrey's, what's our excuse for not embracing each moment in the day?

If we open ourselves to the wonder of laughter in the midst of pain, we create more life.

If we open ourselves to the moment we learn or experience something new by pausing, taking a deep breath, perhaps uttering a blessing to mark that moment, we create more life.

If we open ourselves each day to something so seemingly small as a fresh-scrubbed poem, a moment of meditation, a good meal with family or friends, someone's joyous grin, we create more life.

When we celebrate our miracle moments, we create more life.

∼

Make the miracle of Geoffrey's spirit, and others like him, a living part of each day.

How?

By being open to the elixir of life we possess in each moment.

And even more, by not wasting a single drop.

The Goddess winfrey

Oprah Winfrey is divine.

Some of you may have thought it, perhaps long suspected it. Well, there, I've said it.

Now if you interpret *divine* to mean that she's a modern-day goddess, I can see it. After all, when she speaks, people listen. She sets down guidelines that members of her audience definitely follow. Some might even interpret the devotion paid to her by certain followers of her show, magazine, and personal appearances as akin to worship. Maybe so, but it misses the point.

When I call Oprah divine I'm referring to the fact that, like celestial lights sparkling bright against the night sky, she provides many an observer with the gift of direction. The guiding light she embodies is a lodestar for many, a reference point for values and self-appreciation in a society full of degrading views of what is truly human and sacred.

It wasn't always so. At one time Oprah played the slash-and-burn talk show game as well as the next Sally or Jerry. Some would say even better. She'd air marital disputes, he said/she said confrontations, and testimonials to rage and misfortune, following the accepted view that people hunger for nothing more than to be voyeurs to human misery.

But somewhere in the midst of all that wringing of psychic despair, Oprah came to the conclusion that she could use her personal power to far better advantage for her audience by showing them that to which they could aspire. She began filling her shows with topics and speakers who could rally the human spirit, not subvert it. She and her staff arranged shows on topics dealing with fulfilling your dreams, not destroying them, and they began providing tools for the actualizing of the individual, the galvanizing of the heart. Many critics thought this accent on the positive, this radicalizing of television and public discourse, would send Oprah's ratings plummeting. But to think this is to undervalue the human intellect as well as the human spirit.

What Oprah proves today is that by opening a space for a dialogue of enlightenment, people can and will respond with enthusiasm. They will not only buy the message, they'll make something of it. She illustrates that pandering to the lowest common denominator of humanity is not the only road to success and is not even a desirable one. Her message challenges her audience to find out how good life can be by finding out how good each of us can be. The measure of so powerful a force of nature as Oprah is that she has altered the nature of power.

Think about the way we use our own power on a daily basis. Do we use it to close people down, nipping discussion and ideas—including our own—in the bud? Or do we use it to open up ourselves and others, drawing forth the good each of us has to offer? Do we wield our personal influence to raise the dignity of others, or do we manipulate it to degrade and humiliate?

Born in the humble roots of rejection and a poor self-image, Oprah has managed to open within herself a new way of thinking. Each of us as well is capable of opening ourselves up to the realization that we possess personal power and that we can use it to nourish the spirit within us and others.

~

Each one of us contains sparks of the divine. Whether or not we can open our soul's light to the world determines if we will be vessels of negation or illumination.

The one-in-a-Thousand

There is something about percentages that I have always mistrusted. Statistics strike me as a dispassionate science, turning human data into a series of numbers that, it is said, provide a fairly accurate portrait of the populace. I still like the romance of thinking we are not all quite so predictable, even if our Information Age suggests otherwise. The truth is, it is our very human qualities that allow, at times, for percentages to be turned on their heads, confounding the prognosticators.

I admit, however, to being human and therefore capable of holding contradictory positions. Every so often percentages can appear that portend good news, and suddenly they're my new best friend. When the doctors told us that 99 percent of women who go in for a special prenatal test called a chorionic villus sampling (CVS) display no evidence of abnormalities in the fetus, well, hey, we figured we had it made. The CVS is a highly accurate test given to pregnant women over thirty-five, who, according to medical data, are slightly more prone to birth abnormalities than younger women. It gives prospective parents the opportunity to detect chromosomal defects, such as Down's syndrome, in the first trimester rather than waiting for the more common amniocentesis, which is not administered before the second trimester. For many, the chance to rule out such devastating concerns as early as possible is paramount. The 1 percent of women whose CVS tests come back with evidence of chromosomal damage then have, if so inclined, a choice. But the 99 percent whose tests come back clean as a whistle can indulge in relief and thanksgiving.

Ninety-nine percent! Any gambler, any stock trader, any student, any political candidate, anyone would be beside themselves to get percentages like that.

And then it hits. The shaking of the head and the sad news: we are part of that 1 percent. It's all there in chromosome number twelve, they tell us. The fetus Bonnie is carrying is damaged. It's a statistical certainty. And we shake ourselves in disbelief and hold each other and the tears flow and the dreams hemorrhage and the mourning sets in.

Loving a person as much as I love my wife carries with it the enhanced crush of pain when she dissolves into heartache. And so we begin planning for the inevitable termination of pregnancy at the strong and convincing recommendation of our doctors and genetics counselor. The universe has delivered a *no* to our hopes, and we have to move on. And now we gather the family and friends who don't know what to say. There are promises of beginning again and what good news will come of it next time and how we now have time to take a few more trips and how the percentages favor us in the future and . . .

Out of the clear blue of wonder—a miracle. Our universe tilts on its axis, and we find to our stunned amazement a profound truth: *no* in life doesn't mean forever. And sometimes a *yes* can evolve against all the odds.

Two days after the sad news of the statistical certainty, we get the news that buckles us. The secondary and complete findings are in, and it appears the fetus is almost surely all right after all. It now seems probable that there is some small chromosomal damage in the placenta that will likely prove of no concern. The amniocentesis in another few weeks should confirm what the doctors now believe—the fetus is fine. There will be no termination.

And what are the chances of finding such a result after the preliminary report comes back with its statistical certainty of chromosomal damage?

Point one percent. *One in a thousand.*

Picking ourselves up off the floor, blinking in and out of comprehension, we face the crumbling wall of statistical certainty with disbelief and hearts full of thanksgiving.

It is the eve of Passover. Festival of freedom. Redemption. Renewal of hope. I wonder, what odds were the Israelites given for shaking off the shackles of four hundred years of slavery?

Staying open to hope isn't always easy. The percentages in life can wear us down. But being fully human means that no one can turn us into a statistic, even on our bad days. And sometimes miracles can come in the reopening of a path we thought was closed.

So stay open to the possibility a *no* can turn to *yes*.

~

The one-in-a-thousand proves there's always hope.
Always.

ROOTS RUN DEEP in the HEART

There exists for many of us an idealized version of home, the home almost always remembered through the aching desire to reframe our childhood.

There is also a second version, the actual experience—the real home. It might be the time you backed into the neighbor's car or your sister poured milk over your head in a tumble of laughter, or, for some, it might be the single mental photograph of your parents telling you and your siblings they were getting divorced.

If you are lucky, the two, the ideal and the real, actually coincide. Whatever images and attitudes arise when you think of the place you began to form your sense of self, that place remains significant. Your personal foundation rests on the formation of roots.

In general, those who grow up without a sense of rootedness, or who have failed to acquire roots along the way, are often blown wherever the winds of life take them—unable to hold fast to anything. You know these people. They have a "live by the scruff of the neck" quality. You feel sorry for them when you see them. They teeter more often than most. Then again, perhaps you spotted one of them in the mirror one day and wondered, Who is that person?

Roots grow in all kinds of terrain. They can run deep in the fertile hillside of ideas, in the verdant gardens of religion, in the sacred soil of creativity, in the hollow of one's heart. On a more basic level, roots are simply reflected in the locale where we grew up. *Home* in this context refers to both the natural and communal settings of our youth. For a number of us, this sense of place has been sewn so deep, knit so tightly into our souls that it remains with us on our life's journey no matter where or how far we go.

Vermont is my home.

It has not been my residence for twenty-eight years, and yet it resides within me. It is woven throughout my sense of self.

And the roots weave through memory:

- wondrous winters where, as a child, I would scurry to capture that first snowflake . . .
- tobogganing on Hospital Hill . . .
- sledding down the short embankment across the road from my house . . .
- snowball fights with neighborhood kids, the cold sting of a direct hit . . .
- the artistry of icicles decorating tree and roof . . .
- the buzz of spring and my mother calling us from cartoons to experience the first daffodils pushing their heads out of the earth . . .

- the lazy summers hiking Smuggler's Notch and Camel's Hump . . .
- drinking freely from the water cascading down mountain streams . . .
- the magic startle of grasshoppers popping out of tall grass . . .
- crickets blanketing a summer's night with their communal call . . .
- fireflies dancing—living sparks lighting a child's imagination on fire . . .
- Green Mountains ablaze in gold, russet, orange, and spectacular reds . . .
- jumping wildly in the piles of raked leaves . . .
- ambling down a tree-lined country road on a crisp blue day . . .

I, like many of you, have a lot of homes. My heart is planted in people and places that have touched me in significant and life-affirming ways. When I remember that, when I hug the thought of it, I hold one of life's riches in my soul.

Open up a journal, as well as your heart, and list a few memories that root you in who you are. Get caught in the fertile fields between reality and ideal, and let the images flow. Giving thanks for roots that have served you well is a surefire path to the wonder you deserve.

Now open your mind, and let your imagination run wild.

Think of the ways you are planting new roots. Bless your ability to keep doing so. Think of the ways you are opening wider the door to your soul, allowing life's goodness in. Celebrate both the reality of the home you now have and the ideal of all you would like it to be. Caress the wonder of this moment.

~

I wish you strong roots and an open heart.

Step into . . .

When you get to the end of all the light you know
and it's time to step into the darkness of the
unknown, faith is knowing that one of two things
shall happen: either you will be given something
solid to stand on, or you will be taught how to fly.

BARBARA J. WINTER

Life Can Be *This* Good
When We Step Into

We live in a world of bystanders. Many of us spend our days staring at a computer screen, watching TV, observing and living through the predicaments of others.

When we listen and open ourselves to the gifts of the heart, we have raised our awareness of the goodness that awaits us always. We have tuned ourselves to the sounds and opened a place within our hearts and our lives for wonder to take root.

Now we must move beyond listening, beyond opening, to a place of action. We must *step into* the goodness of life to make it a part of us every day. We discover then that wonder is integral to life and that, in fact, we are capable of generating it ourselves.

Listening provides a connection. *Opening* makes room for the gifts to flow into our hearts. *Stepping into* causes the good to flow out of our hearts and into the world.

In taking an active role, we allow the stories of our lives to sanctify the world with their lessons. These are lessons that we have learned because we have chosen the role, not of bystander, but of participant. We are not satisfied with observing miracles from the outside. We choose to be artists of our own lives. The wonder is in that art.

Stepping into life allows us to get ever closer to fulfilling our promise—to be the best we can be, to grow into our own potential, to become empowered with creativity and meaning.

Step into each day, and bathe in the illumination of its offerings. Add your spark, and the fires of goodness grow.

As you choose a path toward the light, the universe speaks to you, saying, *you* are a light.

coming Around Again

Raising children to adulthood is accomplishment enough for one life, I believe. Guiding them through the shoals of childhood, adolescence, the teen years, and into early adulthood ought to qualify parents for divine dispensation. Or, at the very least, ought to allow us to skip past "Go," collect two hundred dollars, and acquire property on the Boardwalk without having to pay taxes.

My hat is off to all parents who do it and who, in the case of many, do it rather well. The fact that I raised three children for a number of years as a single dad blows my mind. Really. I lie awake sometimes and wonder how I managed it. Actually, a lot of the time, it managed me, but who's quibbling?

In the early 1980s I didn't know any other dad who had primary custody of his children. I knew plenty of divorced families. I think there was a run on divorces in the late seventies and early eighties. Maybe I was simply more attuned to it, since I found myself in the midst of those statistics. Nevertheless, for a good part of my kids' elementary, junior-high, and high-school years it was often me and the other single moms at the ball games and dance lessons and in the doctors' offices.

I could easily feel sorry for myself when it reached midnight and I was doing laundry so my daughter could wear the right blouse for the student assembly or so my son's uniform would be ready for tomorrow's game. I wondered how on earth I was going to manage to attend simultaneously scheduled ball games for two of the kids while getting the third to dance lessons and putting in an appearance at a school project meeting that I was spearheading.

Truth be told, the overwhelming part wasn't logistics. It was spiritual. I hungered for guarantees that my kids knew they were loved completely, unconditionally, and that they had an ample supply of belief in themselves. I prayed constantly that the inner scar of a divorce would heal and that as a family we could transform pain to possibilities. Though I learned to cook some fairly tasty dishes, I cared less about the menu and more about creating a recipe of affirmation for each of my children and me.

And through it all, rather than concentrating on what many of my married and single-without-children friends saw as a Herculean task, I came to know that I was the lucky one. I got to see my kids grow and develop, to tickle their backs at night, to break up the inevitable skirmishes, and to host sleepovers, complete with morning scrambled eggs and bagels. I could whip up that breakfast with the best of them. And as for Band-Aid moments and late-night blues, like many parents, I earned my stripes.

Only now, with my children grown, two of them married

with newborn children of their own, can I stand back and better view the art of it all. Oh, yes, parenting is an art. We paint with our love and our values across the canvas of our children's souls. And there are consequences in the colors we use—the stroke of our brush, the care with which we prepare and execute our vision. We are the lucky ones. Parents and artists.

When I met Bonnie, I knew it would be a wondrous thing to raise a child with her. To do it not alone, but sharing the experience from beginning to end. We would do it together, sharing the art.

People today think I need my head examined, having another kid. Perhaps I do. Then again, I believe in what I do. And I believe in us.

And so, right now, having just become a grandfather twice over, on the cusp of turning fifty, with an energetic stepson, Ari, in tow, Bonnie and I have just welcomed our own little girl. And it seems to me that in choosing to step boldly into the sacred circle of life, I have met my younger self along the way. And so it follows that choices we make along life's path today can reacquaint us with choices we've made years before, in a most life-affirming way.

Just like in Monopoly, I get another turn. And I am filled with gratitude for my older children—Yaffa, Batsheva, and Elisha—for helping to train me. You see, they were the ones who taught me to believe in myself as a parent.

And now, stepping into my role of father anew, I get to pursue the art all over again.

~

Life can be *this* good. Believe it.

The Soul's Aurora

Aurora borealis. I just love the way that jumps off the tongue. It's a voyage of discovery in seven syllables. Certain words take you places by the simple pleasure of their utterance. *Jambalaya* comes to mind, as does *phantasmagorical.* I am not in the same place after pronouncing these words as I was when I began. I've been transported, by the magic of the sound itself.

And then there is the image or emotion conjured by the word. *Aurora borealis* creates a glow. It puts me inside some mystical emanation as it bounces off the roof of my mouth. Seems appropriate, somehow, for a term referring to the northern lights.

Science, of course, is capable of explaining the occurrence of these multicolored light rhythms dancing against the Alaskan sky. Solar storms cast sun particles into the earth's atmosphere, fashioning a magnetic illumination that we see as the flowing fantasia known by the name—yes, say it aloud with me for the sheer joy of it!—*au-ro-ra bo-re-a-lis.*

For the record, a mirror-image light show can be experienced in the southern hemisphere. It's called the aurora australis. The word *australis* fails to fire my imagination to the same extent as good old *borealis.* Which brings me to the hemisphere of the soul.

The boundaries of our physical body can be visually confirmed, but the soul has no such definable borders. Rather, like the northern lights, it ebbs and flows within us, at times barely discernible, at other times bursting forth with illumination that floods our inner terrain.

Why can't we feel that illumination more frequently? For the same reasons most of us in the United States and Europe rarely have an opportunity to glimpse the aurora borealis at all: light pollution and distance. Our need for light is so great that we manufacture it in huge heaping gridfulls. In many of our cities we are so encircled by electric plant-generated light that we literally cannot see the wonder of the stars above us. The opportunity for viewing the real thing has been washed away in society's push for bigger and better.

I'm reminded of the 1994 Los Angeles earthquake, which shook the bejeebers out of those of us living there. A silver lining of the tragedy was the strange and almost mystical sight of my bathrobed neighbors gathering in the electricity-deprived night, staring in wonder up at the heavens as if discovering starlight for the first time.

It strikes me that those who practice impatient living tend to manufacture their own "light," getting a quick fix of artificial stimulus and never leaving room for the natural luminescence of the human gesture. This occurs when we are more focused on high-speed Internet connections than daily-speed people connections. One has to make a conscious choice to hear the kind word or the offer of assistance in our busy Pentium-chip lives. These are the spiritual gifts of human beings logging on to the Internet of life.

By removing the light pollutants that pass for luminosity—the chasing of status rather than sunsets, seeking constant compensation rather than nurturing commitment, having a good time rather than making time for doing good—we clear a path to the soul's ability to illuminate. By stepping into the daily wonder of life's precious gifts found in song, a child's smile, a good book, we allow the light within ourselves to grow stronger.

The size of the aurora depends on how strongly the solar wind hits the earth's magnetic field. Strong gusts kick up particles that allow a wider viewing. A weak solar wind means that only those closest to the magnetic poles are going to catch it. So, too, when the solar wind of wonder is weak within us, we fail to experience the soul's aurora.

Our distance from the prime viewing area of the aurora also determines how frequently we can experience the wonder of their radiance. In Fairbanks and Nome, Alaska, the northern lights are visible almost two hundred days a year. It is our willingness to close the distance between *listening* and *doing* that allows wonder to manifest. Stepping into our lives with the intention of sending life's gifts back out into the world narrows the distance between our soul's aurora and our ability to experience it.

The aurora borealis is a permanent feature of the earth's upper atmosphere. Stepping into the radiance of human interaction and allowing our soul to shine can be a permanent feature of our daily lives, if we want it to be. If we immerse ourselves in the world, body and soul. If we respond to the universe as a celebrant of life.

~

Anyway, I'm heading for Alaska next chance I get. A whole state of people muttering about the aurora borealis. That's heady stuff.

A Different Kind of News

Every time I open up the newspaper or turn on the evening television, I hope for one thing—different news. Well, let me put that another way: I hope for a different *kind* of news. What I'm pining for is something more like . . .

"At the top of our news tonight, the return of autumn—leaves more brilliant than imagination. Stay tuned!"

Or . . .

"Random acts of kindness send the spiritual stock market soaring. Politicians at a loss . . ."

Or maybe . . .

"We interrupt with breaking news: Schoolchildren have gone ballistic, launching a massive Poetry for Shut-Ins Program in a national outpouring of consideration. They have issued a challenge to all citizens to *take up the pen!*"

Hey, I can dream.

Steeped in a plethora of terrorist acts, anthrax exposures, war on foreign soil, and crime reports, arrests, and conflagrations, we are inoculated daily with the terrifying, the really bad, and the ugly. Even when hatred is rooted out, somebody's son or daughter is dying. Oh, yes, every so often a little good news creeps in. But it's rare. And it's hard to blame the journalists, who are just reporting the news, doing their jobs.

Or are they? Are they, instead, practicing selective reporting? I mean, the leaves *are* out there turning. Acts of kindness *do* exist all over, whether a light shines on them or not. Children *are* writing poetry in classes throughout the nation.

I will tell you a lesson I learned, a fairly troubling one, concerning the news business. I learned it from a master politician and someone I considered a very decent man—the late mayor of Los Angeles, Tom Bradley.

It was a brilliant autumn day in L.A. Some seventy-five students and several teachers from the Heschel Day School had made an important and provocative decision. In the previous year a great deal of attention had been paid to the Los Angeles Olympics—constructing new businesses, upgrading facilities, all to showcase the City of Angels before the world. But many felt that little, far too little, had been done for the poor and indigent in the city. And the lack of attention to the human condition was glaring.

Rather than wait for politicians or news agencies to focus attention, the children decided they would lead. They had a strong desire to make a difference. They wrote a song about the need to act, its lyrics expressing idealism and challenges. The teachers and I channeled their enthusiasm into an act of public protest. The plan—to march on City Hall. A children's crusade. To throw, not stones, but ideas. To demand, not political favors, but political leadership.

News stations, the *Los Angeles Times,* Associated Press, and the local weeklies were all duly informed that schoolchildren would be marching on City Hall and would be met there by the mayor. They would deliver a challenge to elevate the lives of the poverty-stricken, the hungry, and the homeless. Furthermore, they had a plan.

A handful of educators and seventy-five junior high students were proposing that businesses and schools adopt a social agency, be paired to form a partnership. Businesses would help with finance and material goods. Schools could provide the human engine, creating a community service component in which students would assist with an after-school workforce that would promote emotional and moral development. Our contingency simply wanted the mayor and political leaders to put some leverage and weight behind the idea.

The group felt that the press coverage of the kids' appearance at City Hall not only would illuminate the need for a major new citywide policy for the poor, it would also expose the children's leadership and, quite frankly, shame business and civic leaders into action. Posters were created, the campaign theme song rehearsed, speeches composed, facts checked and rechecked to ensure credibility.

Finally, the day arrived. Spirits were high. News releases and phone calls had gone out. City Hall, through Mayor

Bradley's office, had proven receptive. It was going to be *some* day for L.A., some special day for seventy-five kids with dreams of making a difference and for the educators anticipating this wondrous occasion when lessons taught would be translated into deeds. Ideas were coalescing into values, and values were being transformed into action in the streets. Was it the echoes of the sixties' protests upon which I'd been weaned that made this all so exciting and passion-filled?

As the bus approached City Hall, our hearts were pumping. A palpable lightening of spirit filled us as we prepared to see television cameras, news reporters, and the press covering this historic meeting of schoolchildren and city leaders. We pulled up, taking to the streets to seize the day. I remember wishing my father and mother were with me, to experience firsthand how the values they had so passionately nurtured in me were now being passed along to the hearts of the next generation.

As we turned the corner onto the City Hall property, I cautioned the kids not to speak to reporters before we had made our presentation to the mayor. With visions of headlines that would shake citizens from their business-as-usual attitude, we approached City Hall. These kids were really doing it. They were really making something of worth happen in this city, and none of us could have been prouder.

But as we rounded the corner, we were struck by the sight

of a plaza filled, not with news vans and photographers but normal everyday passersby and a group of Japanese tourists. As the students and teachers trooped slowly off the bus, realization dawned and silence grew palpable. I watched as they descended the steps and took in the crushing fact that the reporters hadn't shown. Not a one. *Nada.*

The press had passed the story by, and the look on the children's faces would bury Hope itself.

As we drew near to the entrance of City Hall, the door opened and Tom Bradley, a man of his word, emerged. Looking at the children, he was confronted by their sadness. I explained to the mayor that the kids had been told there would be massive press coverage. It was a major story—children challenging the city, becoming a voice for justice, a sign of what's right in the community. Surely we needed such different news to be made in our city, in our world.

Then Bradley gave a cold lesson in the reality of news coverage. Shaking his head, he looked at the assembled sea of idealism and said, "The sad truth is, if you pick up stones and throw them at the windows of City Hall, this would be news—a rebellion they would cover. I'm sorry the press didn't feel it was worthy."

Nevertheless, he insisted they had a message and they should deliver it.

"Who's gonna hear it?" challenged one of the kids.

Bradley smiled, "Well, how about me?"

And with that, the kids leaped into action. They sang their song, delivered their speeches, made their heart-filled case to an audience of one.

Did it make a difference? Yes and no.

They found someone who cared enough to listen. They also learned to distrust adults in the media who had promised to cover so poignant a story but who clearly were nothing more than moths drawn to the hottest news flame.

But could there be a flame hotter than trying to change the world? Hotter than making a difference where a difference was badly needed? Hotter than schoolchildren stepping up and into their community, galvanizing it to lift up the down-trodden?

It may be my naïveté, but it seems to me we could all use more light like that in our world.

Bradley made a difference. So did those kids, bruised dreams and all.

By the way, the lead story that night in Los Angeles had to do with a white-collar worker swindling his company out of thousands of dollars. The second story dealt with a rape. The print press led the next day with the story of an airline strike and a featured report on the deteriorating traffic conditions on area freeways.

The children went on to adopt the Chrysalis Center on

Skid Row in Los Angeles. They led a drive to collect clothing and raise funds so the needy could get a hand up. The agency has sent hundreds of people back to productive lives, and in their own small way, these schoolkids helped make it happen.

Only, the world never knew about it. Work stoppages and strikes apparently made better news copy than the goodness of their hearts. And yet, stepping into a moral void stands beyond headlines.

~

Each one of us who steps in to make a difference in the lives of our fellow human beings makes news of which the universe takes note. For in some small way, we help to tip the balance away from negativity and toward affirmation.

For my money, no matter what made it onto the tube or into print that day, the kids were the real story.

Wherever a different kind of news is celebrated, they still are.

The Perfect Fit

As a child, did you ever have trouble fitting in? If not, do you remember the kid who did? The look on her face? The way he shifted back and forth on the balls of his feet?

I thought about that today when my friend Karen told me about her daughter changing schools because, as one administrator told her, "Your daughter doesn't fit the profile of the kind of student we are developing." Which, according to Karen, was a way of saying they didn't want to deal with students who might actually have to struggle a bit. Her daughter has always done B work. But the school is now billing itself as a college prep institution for the elite and has hired a publicity firm to sell the image. Her daughter made the cardinal sin of pulling a D in math last quarter. Rather than have her take a makeup, hire a tutor, or do extra work, the school prefers she move on where she might "find a better fit."

Karen has shared with me that her daughter, Michelle, has always been a little different. More a loner than a joiner. More Janeane Garofalo than Britney Spears. But always cool in her own way. Obviously not the right kind of cool for an elite school.

With trepidation and high hopes, Karen drove her teen to the new high school, wanting badly for Michelle to feel good about the place. At the end of the first day she was surprised to hear her daughter complain that the school was nice enough but the kids were definitely "not cool." Karen's response was classic: "This year, honey, you're going to have to look beyond cool."

Contemplating what it's like for kids to fit in gets me thinking that the same holds true for grown-ups. Some of us never quite get our footing in the adult world. We are tentative about choices, inhibited when it comes to social settings, unsure of developing or committing to relationships. It's as if everyone else passed the test and got their license to operate in the adult world, and we're still trying to read the instruction manual.

And if this description doesn't fit us personally, perhaps it describes a friend, a relative, or someone we're interested in, a colleague or possible mate in whose potential we believe.

It's one thing to deal with fitting in while navigating the waters of adolescence. That's a time for figuring out your place among your peers or slowly learning which in the array of choices feels right. It's a time of developing and, for many, a period of growth and shaping that gives way to maturity and responsibility. When you are working to fit in as a grown-up, you carry with you years of attitudes and habits that have taken root and can prove more challenging to adjust. But not impossible, by any means. We are all works in progress.

The trick to overcoming what may appear to be overwhelming obstacles of insecurity, awkwardness, and fear of choices is to reframe the challenge. People speak of the quest for healthy relationships, meaningful jobs, or successful life choices as a search for the "perfect fit." Many put off taking a chance on romance or pursuing a job because they think all their ducks are not lined up in a row. But the "perfect fit," like the "perfect mate" or the "perfect job," is a myth, out there alongside "weight loss guaranteed" and "one size fits all."

The challenge is not how to find perfection or discover where exactly each of us fits in to this world. The challenge, instead, is to see how what we have to offer the world is indispensable, an individual contribution we alone can make. The question is not how we *fit in* but rather how we *make the world more fit*—more truthful, more filled with the poetry of personhood, including ours. Some of us are apprehensive about making so personal a contribution, as if it were a power we dare not wield. As Marianne Williamson has stated so beautifully in her book *A Return to Love,* "Our deepest fear is not that we are inadequate. Our deepest fear is that we are powerful beyond measure."

And so, just as Karen was forced to find a new path for her daughter, and just as Michelle was admonished to "look beyond cool," we who would make the journey to a new setting must reframe the route we are to take. It is a journey within, a path to understanding our own uniqueness and spiritual power. Ralph Waldo Emerson said, "The only thing of value in the world is an active soul." So let's begin there. And as with every journey, the toughest part is the first step.

In our quest to make the world more fit, more complete and soulful, we begin by stepping into our own soul, appreciating the gifts of our particular perspective. We rejoice in the way we value a piece of art or can learn different languages. We revel in the kinds of words that move us, the movies that get us thinking, the people who touch our hearts.

We begin by stepping into our soul's universe, examining the way it has been hurt and the times it has felt healed. What healing touch was that? What image or caress or experience nourished it?

We begin by *stepping into* our soul's truth, finding out how our actions can be more *in step* with our beliefs. Taking time to marinate in the goodness we find there. Determining how this quality might emanate from us, imbuing our daily lives with an aura of meaning.

This *stepping into* may lead us to change course. If so, it is cause for celebration. By reframing the challenge before us as seeking, not perfection, but illumination, we alter our approach to living. And as Thich Nhat Hanh observes, "If we don't change our daily lives, we cannot change the world."

~

Now that kind of change is beyond cool.

A Brother in Deed

For many years my brother Mark was an enigma to me. Ten years older, he was a product of my mother's first marriage. His dad, Dr. Harold Levin, had sadly died at the age of forty-four, leaving my mother, a twenty-nine-year-old widow, with the daunting task of raising two young boys, Mark and Michael. She would have help in the person of my dad, whom she would marry a few years later, and she would give birth to me and my sister in quick succession.

I watched my older brothers grow into their teens. Michael seemed to have his wits about him, while Mark seemed angry, willing to take on anyone and everyone. Maybe that comes from losing your daddy at six years old. Maybe not. All I knew was, I both worshipped and feared him.

He played football like a force of nature and proved impervious to pain. I remember the time that his crosstown rivals targeted him, as star fullback of the Burlington High football team, for special punishment. Six members of the opposing team's defense went at him in a succession of hits like something out of *The Godfather*.

A stretcher was dispatched as all of us stood reeling. Whistles were blowing like a traffic jam. As Mark was lifted up, his face covered in blood, my sister and I rushed to our parents, who were hanging over the stands straining for any news on his condition. We were both crying loudly, our voices ringing out above the spectators who peered down in horrified silence as Mark's form was hoisted to the sidelines. At that moment, with the team doctor rushing to Mark's aid, our parents biting their lips with concern, and the stadium standing in hushed curiosity, our brother managed to push himself up on one bloody elbow and scream in my parents' direction, "Shut those brats the hell up!"

You're eight years old, having witnessed the decimation of your brother by a pack of shoulder-padded goons, and you're crying your little heart out. But the object of your anxiety doesn't turn on the refs, he doesn't scream out at his crosstown rivals. No. He turns on his pitiful little whimpering sister and brother—and in front of a thousand witnesses. Go figure. Bloodied and defiant, he insisted on being put back in the game, where he scored the winning touchdown, dragging three opponents with him as he crossed the goal line.

Our father had adopted Mark and Michael when he married Mom, giving them the presence of a caring dad. He honored the memory of Mark's father but freely provided love, guidance, and direction when needed. I can remember the police bringing my teenage brother home in the middle of the night after one of his fights. I could hear the firmness with which Dad talked to Mark, urging him on a less defiant path. Then the tears and the hugs of a father's love would follow. But Mark was not easy to hug. He would pull back, retreat, as if from a memory. He left home when I was ten and, for the most part, was absent from my life until my adult years.

I didn't really come to know my brother until my father neared death. And then, to my great surprise, there was revealed a miracle of a person I had never had the opportunity to know.

Dad suffered during the last years of his life with emphysema. This vital, energetic man was reduced to gasping for breath and often resorted to a mask tethered to the small cylinder of oxygen he came to require. Traveling, of course, was out of the question, as walking took too much of his strength. And yet, Mark would not allow this rival in the guise of ill health to bring Dad down. The thought of Dad being incapable of experiencing life was not acceptable. He simply would not take *no* for an answer.

Mark flew Mom and Dad to Hawaii, where he was then living. He arranged for an apartment near his own. He would shop for them, pick them up at lunch, and take them out each day, always driving right up to any restaurant or scenery so that my father could make it more easily. Moving toward the end of his life, our dad was not going to lose out on experiencing something so beautiful as Hawaii. Mark would give him the experience of drinking deep from life's well exactly when that well appeared to be dry.

Every day for two months, Mark escorted Dad and Mom around the island of Oahu. He opened new vistas, unveiled the hills and valleys and wondrous ocean surrounding the island. Colors my father had never seen formed veritable rainbows of splendor. This gift of time and care and love also renewed Mom. She had been confined with Dad and his illness in their Vermont home, and his ill health had taken a toll on her as well. Now she, too, could reopen to life in the bounty of Hawaii.

My brother had evolved from an isolationist who beat his own angry drum into a man who made symphonies possible for his father and mother. He gave of himself like many never do, and I saw something beyond precious in the way he infused heartache with hope.

At the end of one of the final days they were to spend in Hawaii, Mark took our parents out for a sunset drive along the ocean. He drove them up to the hill overlooking a volcano just as the sun was setting. Our dad was not having a particularly good day, even by what by then had become a difficult standard. But the sight of ocean and volcano and sun breaking into gold and rose hues was irresistible. Dad strained to see beyond the confines of the car window, frustrated that he could not experience all 360 degrees of the natural wonder.

He wanted one more feel of the air wafting across his body, and Mark would make it possible. This brother of mine, this enigma who had always seemed untouchable, lifted Dad into his arms and, cradling him gently, carried him out to the end of the hill. Ocean and sunset lay in splendor before them; the volcano's majestic head was bathed in light. Our father drank in the beauty, the colors, the blessing of if all.

Each one of us can give that gift of life and light by stepping into another's darkness. Family and friends who have isolated themselves may find their way back into our lives. People we thought we knew may surprise us with a depth and compassion we'd never imagined. And at such moments we are able to see how very good life can be.

Because the human spirit has been celebrated.

Finding unrevealed beauty in people proves that the past never equals the future. And stepping into tomorrow is not a matter of simply living, it's an opportunity for loving.

tzimtzum

According to Jewish tradition, God set about creating the world, fashioning heaven and earth, oceans and rivers, wild grass and herb-bearing seeds, trees of maple and palm, hills and valleys, birds of all designs, animals of every persuasion. And through and around all of this creation God fired off an effusion of light.

Now by *effusion of light* I don't mean some rapturous rays of sun or cascades of moonbeams. We're talking here about *luminus maximus,* an entire universe filled to the brim with golden sustenance, the heady intoxicating wine of divine illumination.

The problem with all this glowing glory can be stated quite simply—too much of a good thing. God took a step back, surveyed all of creation, and realized, Oops! No room for the pièce de résistance. With all that light filling every viable molecule of creation, there was no place left for Woman and Man.

Major design flaw.

What to do?

The Creator thinks and thinks, tossing out one idea after another, before finally hitting upon the only credible solution: God must remove *God.*

In order to make room for the living creatures who would

become known as partners in the ongoing work of creation (that's you and me, gang), the Creative Spirit opts to retract some of her own brand of effusive light. God chooses to remove some of God to make room for the rest of us. Pretty major, wouldn't you say? This process of voluntarily pulling back divine illumination to allow the rest of us to exist is known in rabbinic teaching as *tzimtzum.*

It occurs to me that we might learn something from this sort of personal sacrifice. There are times when we become so self-absorbed, so wrapped in our own light, that there is no room for others. Our world is brimming over with our own luminosity, and we're quite taken with the glow. At times like these, spouses, partners, children, friends, and coworkers all search in vain for a place to fit their concerns in the roiling orbit of our daily planet.

At such a juncture, if we have managed to stay in tune with even a fragment of awareness, we come to realize what we must do. But if you're like me, it will more likely take someone close to you, calling you on the proverbial carpet.

Such intervals may indeed coincide with a supernova burst of personal creative energy, but if we can pause, dial back the music, and retract a bit of our light, we will allow others who are integral to our life to step into our universe.

It is a miracle of the spirit, this individual tzimtzum. In choosing to carve out of our own personal territory the terra firma upon which others can interact, we step into a whole new world of blessing; we elevate *self*-awareness to *human*-awareness. In doing so, we experience more fully the wonder of friendship, the joy that comes from being one part of the whole.

Removing some of our frantic busyness leads us to new vistas of wonder. It allows the light of others to shine, revealing how good life can be when it's shared.

~

Too much light. Hmmm.

Las Vegas could definitely benefit from a little tzimtzum. You think?

Baby Talk

What is it about a newborn baby that turns perfectly sane folk into cooing, tongue-clucking, head-bobbing, blithering block-heads?

Count me among them. I hold my nine-week-old daughter as often as possible and find myself inventing a whole new language in the process. We look each other up and down, some sort of primitive salutation. Having made a positive and acceptable ID, the two of us begin a conversation to which no one else in the world is privy and, even if they were, would find impossible to decode.

Out of her rosebud of a mouth come gurgles and hiccups and spitballs and a strange sort of magical noise that sounds like a giggle in reverse. It starts off as a tiny laugh then immediately gets sucked back into her throat as if she couldn't bear to part with it. I must also be prepared, in the midst of our discourse, for a cascade of generous portions of her last feeding, which she upchucks with so sweet a face you practically welcome the experience.

But the real discovery here is what comes out of my own mug. I mean the E.T.-like alien tones pitched often at decibel peaks to which only babies and canines can ascend. I've addressed thousands of people in public settings over the years, but no one could possibly identify that man with the one emitting squeaks and snorts when engaged in baby daughter-daddy dialogue.

I have begun to think that the whole cooing thing is actually a cosmic test. Babies, still in touch with the source of primal wonder, are checking our ability to abandon all artifice, drop the stilted everyday conversation, and carry on consequential communication. And, of course, allowing us to feel we're the ones in control while they teach us how to play all over again.

Believe it or not, a completely unscientific study—my own—shows that roughly 67 percent of us, fully two-thirds, are still capable of producing completely unintelligible talk when confronted by the tiniest versions of ourselves. So, you know, there's hope for the species.

Something else has caught my attention. My daughter can be carrying on a perfectly delightful series of chortles punctuated by the occasional spit bubble, when all of a sudden—shades of Jekyll and Hyde—she bursts into a fireball of frustration, caterwauling in a crimson tantrum that puts alley cats to shame.

The sudden flood of tears seemingly conjured from thin air, the facial contortions that strike you with an immediate flush of guilt, not to mention the awe-inspiring assault on your adult eardrums, is mitigated, if at all, by your fumbling, haphazard attempts to tranquilize the beast that a minute ago was your bouncing baby girl.

So you turn her this way and that. You erupt in a rapid-fire volley of grunts and squawks meant to short-circuit the tantrum and reestablish sanity. And then, grasping for miracles, you manage to unearth a binky—yes, a pacifier—buried under a chair cushion, and your world is restored.

I ask my wife about this. How can our baby's sweet dimples and creamy disposition so wholly transform into the Twilight Zone? Without skipping a beat, she responds, "She's just like me."

This gets me thinking. Maybe she's just like all of us. Me and you and the guy trading on the floor of the stock exchange. (Talk about your tantrums and alien behavior!) The overworked college kid selling me tension along with my coffee in the morning rush is the same young man who will mellow out in an afternoon yoga class. The hard-pressed cop blowing her gasket as she tries to weather the wild horns and keep the traffic moving is the same woman who will later celebrate a candlelit anniversary dinner with her husband. And the quiet librarian who helps me locate an obscure copy of Renaissance poetry is the same fellow who that evening will let fly a slew of bloodcurdling shrieks while kicking butt at karate before going home to soak in classical music and candlelight.

We all have the ability to daily transform ourselves from gentle and sweet to wild and wacky. It's part of stepping into the thick of life with all its pulls and tugs, tantrums and triumphs. It can happen like *that*. I guess it means we're human. Babies remind us of that, too.

~

Maybe one of the secrets to living a life *this* good is to step into our lives with playful wonder, even if it takes a refresher course. That way we're reminded that there is humanity in the rhythm of our many moods.

This much I know: when all else fails, try the binky.

An Angel in the Capital

Over the years, in my capacity as an educator, I have helped lead groups of teenagers in their first visit to our nation's capital. One of the most moving experiences of any visit is, inevitably, a stop at the Lincoln Memorial, a short walk from the Vietnam War Memorial—the Wall.

I never tire of commenting on the emotional ties connecting us to this American corner of history. As we stand on the steps leading to the monolithic statue of our sixteenth president, I always speak about Marian Anderson. The Daughters of the American Revolution had turned Anderson away from performing at their hall because of the color of her skin. The First Lady, Eleanor Roosevelt, a woman who knew something about justice and values, stood by the singer in support as Anderson gave her concert from these steps as a protest against intolerance. Each woman embodied courage and chutzpah in equal measure. Would that contemporary politicians possessed the backbone of these women!

Recently I was in Washington, delivering my talk to a group of students, when I found myself pausing in the middle of my speech about Mrs. Roosevelt. Lifting my head, I looked to my left, and the Wall seemed to look back at me with silent, dark eyes. Addressing no one in particular, I launched into an open-ended contemplation of an intimate sadness.

I spoke of growing up in the sixties, where the unsettling reality of being sent off to war coexisted with attaining puberty. I told of the draft and the terrifying feeling of watching on television every night of your teenage life the images of war and killing and destruction. I told of getting a deferment on account of pursuing a higher education while many young men, the poor and the minorities, were sent off to do their duty. I expressed the heartache of hearing about one of my classmates, a kid from the wrong side of the tracks, a jock who had once beaten me up, who had been so sure he was going to find his future in the rice fields of Vietnam. He would return a war hero, he confided, and then he'd be *somebody*. Harmie was blown up in one of those rice fields. They buried him in the cemetery just over the centerfield fence of our high school where he had known athletic glory. He was here in this place, his name over there on the Wall.

Looking up, I saw the faces of my students, genuine concern and tears in their eyes and—but where had they all come from? Suddenly I was aware we were not alone. Lost in my thoughts and pain and passion, I had failed to notice a sizable gathering of tourists eavesdropping on my rant about Vietnam and Harmie and the price of war and the heartache of guilt over having been spared the fighting.

Sobered by the strangers listening to my deepest passions, I bowed my head and, muttering something, slipped off the steps and began making my way toward the Wall.

I'm not sure what caused me to stop, but slowly I came to a halt and turned to look back at the crowd. The strangers who'd been drawn in by this open confessional as well as my group of kids and fellow educators all had remained in place as if glued by some secret force.

And then I saw him.

It was as if a sea of people had parted, and from deep within the crowd this man appeared. He was husky, African American, about my age. And to my astonishment, he was now running straight for me. And I was unalarmed. I watched him hurl himself across the open plaza that separated us, his face filled with emotion. Out of the corner of my eye I could see my students, astonished, not knowing what was about to happen. And still the man kept coming, and still I didn't move but witnessed it all as if outside myself.

As the man covered the last few yards in what seemed like slow motion, his arms suddenly flew open from his sides like giant wings. He was about to encompass me, and still I stood my ground. The moment seemed suspended, as if the universe was calling special attention to its details. A second later he enveloped me, and I felt as if I was melting . . . melting into the arms of an angel.

Pulling me close, tears flowing, an inner ache clutching at

his throat, he held me. After a few seconds he whispered into my ear what seemed a prayer of thanksgiving: "You spoke my heart. You spoke my heart. Thank you. God bless you."

At this embrace, something inside of me just welled up and poured out. I simply let the tears go. Students, colleagues, and perfect strangers stood transfixed as two men, one black, one white, held each other on the concrete bridge connecting the Lincoln Memorial and the Vietnam Wall. Images of war and protests and a racial divide raced through me as I heard the stranger comforting me through my tears. "It's all right, man, it's all right, I know," he said, and he rocked me.

After a moment I let out an enormous sigh, the kind that follows a cleansing cry. He smiled warmly with a nod of connection. He looked at me for another second, as if he might say something more. We separated without another word. He slipped away, back into an anonymous crowd, and, as quickly as he'd appeared, was gone.

I looked up to see the Wall. Only now it appeared to me as two massive black wings opened wide, embracing those who would come to visit, to remember, to pray. I knew I had let go of something at that moment. And something had let go of me.

～

Students tell me they will never forget what they witnessed that day. As for me, though I find Washington's grand monuments and documents of history moving, the highlight of my D.C. experience no longer resides in paper and stone. More stirring to my blood is the memory of a human angel, appearing out of nowhere, in the valley of my distress.

Holding me. Healing me. Quieting my heart.

This person, this angel, did not simply observe the moment of my pain. He felt it and chose to step into the middle of it. Because the human touch can heal. Because we need to step into each other's lives if for no other reason than we can bring comfort and compassion by doing so.

Such a gift restores us all.

A Human Oasis

About every two or three months I find myself in a section of the city where a certain laid-back restaurant occupies a busy corner. It may not be the food that draws me in so much as the bohemian atmosphere—a mix of rock and jazz on the sound system, classic comfy booths, avant-garde lighting fixtures that hang low from an art-covered ceiling, and, most important, a hands-off policy among the staff. You can sit and read the paper, catch up on your bills, compose a poem, or simply relax.

One of the joys of checking into this easygoing oasis is being greeted by the same waitress, an upbeat woman in her late thirties, a face full of freckles looking fresh out of Ireland. No matter how long it's been since my last visit, the woman's cheerful greeting is always the same—a generous smile and a listing of what she knows I want. My order never changes, but she repeats it just to make sure I haven't slipped the habit: "omelette, easy on the oil, tomatoes, bagel, onion if we have it, otherwise plain, coffee, ice water with lemon, that right?" Yup, that's me. And I'm secretly grateful each time that she remembers. It's a little taste of familiarity in a large and sprawling metropolis.

One of the hallmarks of this long-standing interaction is

how little we actually say to each other. There's the acknowledgment of welcome, the "how have you been?" pleasantries, and, of course, that order ritual. She leaves me alone to read or write yet somehow magically appears at the precise moment I look up for a refill. It's uncanny. But who is this person, really? And why, out of the several wait staff in this funky eatery, do I connect with her, even if in a fairly limited fashion?

The last time I was in we ran through the ritual, only this time I laughed at myself for being such a creature of habit that there exists a person in the universe who sees my face and thinks immediately, *omelette*. She grinned and said something about enjoying her regulars. I pointed out that at a clip of every couple of months I could hardly be considered a regular. She countered by giving me a little gem: "It's not the frequency, it's the friendliness."

There's a world of wisdom in that observation. No matter how often we run into people who are on the periphery of our lives, it's the act of a genuine smile, an attitude of appreciation that we may even come to count on that makes the human interchange a memorable one. To offer up that kind of greeting with friendly familiarity as opposed to perfunctory precision is key to our stepping into the world like we mean it.

Speaking briefly with her, I found out the woman is engaged to a furniture designer who handcrafts his creations. I shared photos of my family and was surprised to hear that she knew the very town in Ireland where my wife and I had experienced the most intense sunset—but not because she was Irish. Rather, it was because her father had been a passionate golfer and had dragged the family to the best golf courses all over the world. Lahinch had been part of the European tour. I learned that she is a painter and uses all of her tip money to buy materials for this passion. That she dreams of setting up a studio and considers Georgia O'Keeffe one of her life's inspirations.

I was almost embarrassed that this artist was serving me up a breakfast. She should be out there following her heart, using her talent on a canvas. She may have suspected my thoughts, for in the next moment she gave me one more gift of counsel: "Art comes from living, not the other way around."

By stepping into the world with passion, we all become artists of life. It may be that we're drawn to certain human beings because we unconsciously sense the art in their living. Or it just could mean that in the hustle and bustle of our high-speed lives, someone who graciously remembers something so basic as your food preferences is herself an oasis of humanity.

$\sim$

In stepping into our daily lives, the words of this woman-waitress-painter-artist could hang on our soul's doorknob:

It's not the frequency, it's the friendliness.
Art comes from living, not the other way around.

I left a really big tip.

Receive...

Whatever we are waiting for—peace of mind, contentment, grace, the inner awareness of simple abundance—it will surely come to us, but only when we are ready to receive it with an open and grateful heart.

SARAH BAN BREATHNACH

Life Can Be *This* Good
When We Receive

We *listen* and we hear the call of life. We *open* ourselves and the call becomes a song rooted within us. We *step into* the world with that song and the song becomes a blessing.

In placing that blessing into the world, we now come to *receive* the full measure of wonder we deserve, for the universe responds, measure for measure, wonder for wonder.

The moments in our daily lives that remind us of being more human, not less; that call us to be sacred beings, not profane; that grant more life, not its antithesis—these are the gifts that teach us how good life can be. They anchor us in a sea of instability and envelop us in wings of inspiration.

Taking a few moments each day to reflect upon the people with whom you've interacted, the places you've been, or the ways you've grown allows you to receive beauty that often goes unnoticed.

We are glorious creatures, capable of great goodness. We are, each of us, deserving of wonder.

Reach into the stories of your days, into the hallowed place of blessings—those you've created and those you've received—and you will feel the glory of your own humanity.

That is worthy of celebration. Don't you agree?

And as you *receive* the blessings of the universe, each and every day, pay attention to its gentle whisper: *you* are a wonder.

The Gift at Dawn

My baby, Shira, wakes up in the morning with a smile on her face. From what I can tell, this upbeat greeting of the new day takes place every morning. Imagine that—opening your eyes, seeing the light of a fresh twenty-four hours, and flashing your pearly whites, or rosy gums, in affirmation. And not just once in a great while, but as a daily habit. It's gotten so that I, who love to lie curled up in a ball under the covers, will forgo the pleasure in favor of the powerful blessing of witnessing Shira's awe-producing grin as the dawn kisses her on the cheek.

And this gets me thinking about how we open the gift of each new day. Is the attitude we take into our lives revealed in our faces and our actions when we awaken? Does that grumpy greeting we give to a roommate, to a family member, or to our mirrored selves in the early moments after opening our eyes mean that irritability is our constant companion? Conversely, does a cheery salutation at the sight of morning light indicate a warm and positive nature?

I am sure that the irritable lot of us breaks into a smile every so often and those who seem to find good everywhere are capable of a harsh word now and again. But is the modus operandi of our lives right there in the grunts, groans, or grins we produce at the crack of dawn? And if it is, what manner or method of response best fits the bill if, indeed, we are capable of change?

Maria von Trapp would say one ought to greet each new day with a song. That might come easier to people like her, for whom the hills were alive with the sound of music. And Maria, who in her later years was always referred to as the Baroness, was still known to have a temper no matter what tune she sang at dawn.

My fourth-grade teacher, Mrs. Herschede, believed cleaning out and feeding one's horses before you so much as brushed your own teeth put you in the proper frame of mind to "make something out of your day other than mischief." Of course, none of us in class actually owned a horse, though we'd occasionally ride one at the county fair. Mrs. H, on the other hand, commuted from her country farm, and somehow all of her lessons seemed to come filtered through livestock. It never occurred to her that urging ten-year-olds to build their minds if they wanted to compete with the other horses in the field wasn't much of a motivation. At any rate, I still can't see how shoveling manure first thing off the bat makes for a pleasant day. But, then again, maybe that's just me.

Henry David Thoreau insisted on a good brisk walk, no doubt beneficial for circulation, as soon as he had risen. Now, this custom may be attributed to him only during his days at Walden Pond, where, truth be told, there wasn't a whole heck of a lot else to do. On the other hand, my wife likes a power walk or jog first thing in the morning, which not only is good for conditioning her physically but also proves beneficial to me, as I sprawl across the entire bed for my extra snuggle time while she's doing it.

All in all, there are many ways to greet a new morning, some of them good for the heart, some for the soul. And some of them just filled with an orneriness that broadcasts to the world, Gangway, I'm back in the saddle.

Truth is, I'm not really sure being sweet or grumpy at the sight of morning light sets the theme for what's to follow in your life that day. It occurs to me it just might be the other way around. In other words, how you live your life may set the attitude with which you greet each new day.

The person for whom work is a drag, for whom commitment is a prison fortress to be avoided at all costs, for whom life is an endurance test, has set the framework for each new day. Waking up means having to go through everything abhorrent all over again. Such a person has placed an imprint on his or her psyche that equates *morning* with *warning,* and *getting out of bed* with *that familiar sense of dread.* "Stuck in a rut" for folks like this is a career choice. Clearly, when each day is an excuse for coming up with new excuses, greeting the morning doesn't rank high on the to-do list.

Check out those who live life like it is a broad,

magnificent, white canvas and they own the brushes and paints. They can, Jackson Pollock-like, drip and dance their colors every which way they please. For such people, living a life *this* good is an imperative. They see in responsibility an opportunity to grow. They find meaning even in failure and redouble their efforts to succeed. Such people see dawn as a gift to be received with a joyous heart *because* of its promise.

～

I haven't got this down to a science. The can-do folks might still wake up with a groan, and the can't-do might greet the day with a grin just for the hell of it. All I know for sure is my baby's morning ritual of smiling at the world is a daily gift I get to receive, even imitate—a gift that dirty diapers can never diminish.

The vistas of the soul

Miracles of the human spirit are far and away the apex of wonder. Awe-producing vistas—breathtaking mountains, sensual ocean sunsets, rivers undulating through misty highlands—heighten our awareness of the majesty of nature. But viewing the grandeur of the human spirit heightens our awareness of the majesty of the soul. Sometimes we see it in people who volunteer for tasks that benefit those in dire need—serving the hungry or victims of disaster or children in desolation. We find it in firefighters, rescue workers, and caregivers. Other times we come face-to-face with this affirmation in our own circle, in the extraordinary gifts and sacrifices of the heart made by a loved one. Every so often, we come across it in public figures who shake the world by risking everything for a greater cause.

I was a reluctant dinner guest at a Los Angeles affair, the kind of political soirée that I try to avoid by any means possible. To my delighted surprise, however, on this beautiful summer evening outdoors, on a glorious sunset of a night, I was introduced to another guest at the dinner, Mrs. Jihan Sadat, the widow of the murdered Egyptian president. We exchanged a brief greeting and moved on. This woman has known such pain, I thought, and yet manages to carry herself with enormous grace. Imagine how moved I was, as luck would have it, that while strolling on the far side of the lawn, taking in the sunset sometime later, I found Mrs. Sadat there, away from the crowd. Barely aware of a few others now drawing near, I took the opportunity to tell her how much I admired her husband. I asked her what she was now doing, and she spoke of her work at the University of Maryland where she taught, spending half her time here in the U.S., the other portion of the year back in Egypt.

I told her I had been overwhelmed by her husband's visit to Jerusalem years earlier. As president of Egypt, he had been the leader of the Arab world in its stand against Israel. He had led that contingency in wars against the Jewish state. And then, in a remarkable evolution of the human spirit, he determined to risk everything, not for war, but for peace.

Now, I'm sure Mrs. Sadat had heard this many times, from people in all walks of life. And maybe something in my voice or in the sunset spoke to her, but what she did next astonished me. Drawing me into her confidence, she looked at me with an enormous warmth kissed by sadness and said, "Shall I tell you how it happened?"

I believe I didn't even respond. My mouth simply parted in wonder as she told me a story at once remarkably intimate and profoundly prophetic.

She told me of the day her children had come running into

her bedroom in the late afternoon with a cry, "Mama, Mama, Papa is going to Jerusalem." They were breathless, she said, and alarmed, as was she. In the next instant, Anwar, her husband, came in. She immediately rushed to him, worry blanketing her face.

"Anwar, tell me it's not true. It cannot be true!"

"But it is, my sweetest," he said, quite simply. "I must do this."

And with a knowledge both terrible and assured, Jihan Sadat whispered, "But my darling, they will kill you."

She told me that she was fully aware of the fact that extremists in her own country would never allow their leader to make peace with an ancient enemy without reprisal.

What happened next in the privacy of their bedroom Mrs. Sadat conveyed to me with a faraway bittersweetness in her eyes, as if she were looking at her husband at that moment and he at her. She told me Sadat gathered her in his arms with love and certainty.

"Then I would have died for peace, Jihan," he said, and held her as if he'd never let go.

She told me that when her husband returned from his historic visit to Jerusalem, a visit that had shaken ancient enmity to its core, replacing it with the awe of possibilities, he was on fire with joy. He'd rushed to show her the banners made for him by Israeli children who had greeted him with cheers and kisses. The banners contained Israeli and Egyptian flags, side by side, as if they were one. He told her he had seen tomorrow in their eyes and that, other than his marriage to her and the birth of their children, it had been the most miraculous event of his life.

Anwar Sadat was gunned down in a hail of bullets a short time later, felled by terrorists among his own people, as Jihan had predicted. He had died for peace.

As I looked into his widow's eyes, I received this incredible woman's grace. For some unfathomable reason and the kiss of serendipity, I had been allowed to hear, from a participant in history, something that would never be mentioned in history books—the intimate exchange between husband and wife, of vision and courage and of the certain knowledge of what it would cost.

Sadat's bravery transcended war.

It transcended the steel grip of the shackles of hatred.

It gave birth to a dream of peace, a dream that still lives in all people of goodwill.

~

I have thought long and often of this meeting—of how the human spirit can come to cast out hatred and receive a gift of love and the grace to practice it in return. And that if each of us would search our souls, we might find there vestiges of old wars that do nothing more than make us feel old. Tired. Uninspired.

In allowing love to grow, we are capable of a greatness of human connection that imbues life with *goodness*. We can renew our vision and, where there is division, provide the courage to make life whole. Sadly, the world has recently witnessed a new brand of mortal enemy. Such enemies wield the weapon of hate with religious fervor. Sadat would recognize this hatred. Yet, it is also true that in our individual lives, we often possess an enemy that lies within, battered by old conflicts yet unsure how to leave them behind.

Bold action means resolving to change, moving from stubborn struggle to the redemption of acceptance and love. It is a gift we receive every time we decide that harboring ill will and intolerance makes our soul pay too heavy a price. Truly living means allowing for our soul's growth.

And it follows that life can be *this* good only when there's goodness in it.

Direction Signals

You know those times you're driving along in your car—mind wandering off somewhere, thinking over some snippet of dialogue you recently had with a friend or mate, some piece of business that needs tending, daydreaming about a trip or a promotion or the person on the billboard up ahead—and someone honks or you hear the little click-click-click and suddenly become aware that your direction signal is on and probably has been on for some time? You quickly flip it off, look around slightly embarrassed, and return your attention to the road, all eyes and ears and taillights.

Maybe, while we're busy driving our cars, consciously or unconsciously, we're also busy sorting through the things that drive us. Maybe anytime we're on autopilot—standing in line at the grocery store, riding an elevator, working out, or waking up—a beehive of processing is taking place within that could make a Madonna concert look like a tea party.

Which is why, when you think about it—and usually we can't help ourselves—the mind, with its accompanying attention and alertness, sometimes simply crashes from exhaustion. It's working a heavy load. That's why a vacation is so necessary—but preferably not while operating a vehicle.

Now music is a definite option here. The mind can ride the

wave of a sound or melody. A psychic letting go kicks in and a restorative energy fills us when we allow the mind to slow down and glide along more calmly. Silence, whether during a yoga pose or simple breathing exercise, can likewise slow the speeding vehicle of the mind. I have found in such moments of quiet that I can hear a voice inside me that is often drowned out in an assault of information.

But there's another way to give the mind a break from its occupation with business and busyness, and that's laughter. I get a dose of Elayne Boosler or Steve Martin, and I'm a goner. Margaret Cho has broken me up with her one-liners on being Korean American. And I can still completely lose it at the frenetic antics of Robin Williams.

Humor isn't solely in the domain of the professional comedian. Friends and family can provide rich fodder. I once became unhinged with fits of laughter, tears streaming down my face, the time my buddy David called from Vermont to tell me he had hiccuped and thrown his neck out. That image still sends me into hysterics. Or the way my friend Jane breaks into an impish grin when her attempt to help an acquaintance lands her in hot water. Her words—"no good deed goes unpunished"—coax a knowing laughter from me. Then there's the way my wife tells a joke with the punchline from a completely unrelated joke. You gotta love it.

But of course what we all need from time to time, to get

away from all the psychic maneuvering that goes on in the cerebellum, is a good laugh at ourselves. I get it when my colleague Bill greets me by lowering his head in mock solemnity with the words "O rabbinical one, I bow to the divine within you." I got a good one the time I was giving a particularly morose and long-winded talk and my friend Charlie, sharing the stage, slipped me a note on the podium that read, "Just because you had a bad day doesn't mean I have to suffer."

Take a moment to think about the people in your life who provide the laughter. Be sure to fold yourself into the mix. Being able to appreciate the humor in our lives allows us to refresh the mind by receiving new directions.

~

You see, I'm not wholly convinced that those direction signals we fail to turn off are always mistakes. It may be, indeed, that our mind is letting us know that we want to change the direction we're headed in. Laughter is clearly a road map to less stressful living. Taking life so seriously is not only exhausting to the mind, it's exhausting to the spirit. The soul needs to receive some lightness of being to renew its purpose. And we need to pay heed to the signals we receive from the universe. They may be letting us know that we can get lost when the directions in which we're headed are too busy and unclear.

As Jane Wagner puts it, "All my life I wanted to be somebody. Now I see I should have been more specific."

Heart Photos

As I sit in the warp and woof of my ever-changing life, I become more and more aware of the power of photographs to move me—people and places, captured in a moment of time, for all time. I can come upon a photographic portrait of a family I have never laid eyes on before and be moved to tears. Something in the visible statement of generations connected forever, in the poetry of images hugged together and kissed onto a negative, which, of course, becomes a positive when developed.

When you're little, you delight in photographs, particularly if you're in them. Usually *only* if you're in them. "Where's me? Where's me?" I'm sure I said. I know my kids did. My stepson, Ari, can sit for hours looking at photos, as long as the photos feature that one singular face.

Photographs can never replace the actual experience. But they can serve as agitators to the pulse of memory. Sometimes a particular photograph allows us to revisit something or someone we thought we knew, only to find our memory has played tricks on us. All in all, photographs help set the record straight. They have the power to reveal a texture, a deeper layer, taking a moment frozen in time and thawing it before our very eyes.

I have been shaken to the core of my being by an Ansel Adams or brought to giddy laughter by the work of Annie Leibowitz or, for that matter, touched with the impish mirth of the work of Anne Geddes with those infants emerging from flower pots. Her image of the tiniest of newborns curling asleep in a father's open palm has stunned me speechless.

Yet, for all the exquisite artistry of such images, I am most profoundly moved by the photographs taken by the heart, captured by the camera within.

We carry *heart photos,* the ones taken of people, places, and moments that have been imprinted on our lives. I have them of each of my children's births. There's one of my father's tears, of the grandfathers I never met but whose images developed inside of me, of my grandmother's home with an accompanying soundtrack of her voice. That's right, her voice. You see, when it comes to heart photos, anything is possible. They come with sound and in all kinds of sizes. At times the characters in them move, like those imagined by J. K. Rowling in her Harry Potter books. Sometimes they appear in ever-changing colors.

They're all there in living splendor and framed with emotion:

- My mother's hand clasping mine as I lay in the hospital following my tonsillectomy

- My brother in high-school football gear
- My other brother in uniform leaving home for military duty
- The Western Wall, my dad melting into the stones as he delivered his prayer
- My mother at her typewriter composing poetry
- Another, of her cradling the first flowers of springtime
- My wedding, under a full October moon in the Vermont birch trees
- A plethora of photos taken by the heart. And to my surprise, the colors never fade

Each of us carries that inner camera with us throughout life. Our film supply is endless. But unlike the photographs printed and developed on paper, these flesh-and-blood photos residing in our soul's library can be seen only by the photographer. We may speak of them, describe them to others, but our eye alone can receive and behold the images we have captured in our respective lives.

～

Each of us is an artist of life. This treasure trove of personal heart photos lives within us. And, yes, it will die with us. But for the precious time we are given to inhabit this life and this earth, we get to pull out the photographs imprinted on our hearts and souls and relive, renew, and *receive* their beauty. That's one heck of an opportunity.

And the kick of it is, heart cameras at the ready, we get to add to our collection every . . . single . . . day.

second impressions

Once while traveling alone in Scotland, I found myself sharing a pint with a feisty elderly woman in a crowded Edinburgh pub. She was dispensing counsel like beer to any within earshot. She didn't think much of the fact that the only part of Scotland I'd managed to see was the monument-strewn confines of its capital. "Here now," the weathered Scotswoman intoned, "you can't much speak o' seein' Scotland lest you've been to the hills."

Now by "the hills," my pub mate meant the Highlands. I was informed it would be a bit of a train ride to the base and then a journey by bus "a wee ways up and beyond." Catching the twinkle in her eye, I surmised that this local character might just know something I didn't, so on to the hills it was the next morning.

Arriving at Inverness, I caught a bus, traveling with a potpourri of other tourists deep into the Highlands. At some point along the way, in the middle of what appeared to be nowhere in particular, the driver pulled the bus to the side of the road. Rather peculiarly, he insisted we get out and take a good look around. Now had this happened in America I might have thought the driver was camouflaging a bus problem of some sort. But, hey, this was the Scottish Highlands.

Maybe he was heeding the call of nature. Who knew? I disembarked.

I immediately understood the need to stop. There, shrouded in a peekaboo mist, was a sight of unmitigated wonder. Bountiful trees danced in a glen, a gurgling stream wended its way through fern and fen. I inhaled the sweet air and let out a small gasp at the glory of this piece of earth. Unknown to me, the driver had caught my gaze and quietly sidled up to share the joy of my discovery. Whispering softly in my ear, he could have been the craggy old pint drinker who'd sent me here: "Aye, laddie, *now* you've seen Scotland."

It gets me thinking. This experience of discovering the real soul of a place is similar to finding the real soul of a person. People may not reveal their beauty, their uniqueness, on first blush. We might have to give them some time, be willing to travel a little further to truly see them.

I had a friend, Leslie, who was once detoured through a rather bleak part of Los Angeles known as the nickel—Fifth Street, part of Skid Row. Less than ten blocks from City Hall, twenty from the majestic Dorothy Chandler Pavilion, it was a section of the city my friend had never entered. Like most Angelenos, if you didn't have to go there, why would you? A series of rundown storefronts, peopled with panhandlers and street people, it was a bleak picture. Now caught in a traffic detour through the underbelly of the city, Leslie was simply praying the detour signs would lead her out just as fast as the lights would take her.

Suddenly her car came to a halt and with it her heart. The car had stalled out. Quickly she gave it the gas, flipping the ignition. Nothing. Looking around at the depressing scene of denizens in dirty clothing hunched in boxes for housing, she redoubled her efforts. Again, no sale. The engine would not respond. Now she panicked. How was she going to get out of here?

And then she saw him—a man in torn clothing and unkempt hair, and he was making his way out into the street and straight for her. Leslie began to hyperventilate, closing all the windows, locking every door. She looked up again. Maybe she was mistaken. Maybe the man was crossing over and would bypass her. No such luck. The wild matted figure with the ripped overcoat was indeed but yards away from her car, only now something else came into view. He was dragging something. Some long meshed bag of who knows what—and my friend's heart rate went into overdrive. This was it. The man was going to pull some weapon, some scrap of metal from that bag, break through the window, that would be it—

Leslie heard the knock on the window and looked up from the gears where her eyes had fallen in silent prayer. She was facing this wild street person who was pointing at his bag then back at the car. He was saying something, but what with

Leslie's windows being closed airtight and the pounding coming from her chest, she couldn't make out what. Suddenly the man went to the front of the car and opened the hood. Reaching into the bag, he pulled out something that looked like pliers and, to my friend's alarm, began tooling around. I should point out that this all occurred before the proliferation of cell phones, or else Leslie, a high-powered attorney, might have had the entire downtown force of the LAPD rushing to her rescue.

Next thing you know, the wild-haired man had taken out Leslie's battery. He again knocked on the window. Leslie thought he was going to—what—attack her, beat her with it? Something awful, at any rate. But the man looked quite serious and, truth be told, rather earnest. Leslie relented and rolled down the window a crack. That's when she heard the words that astounded her: "It's your battery, see? I used to be a mechanic in the army, got down on my luck, but I still know my way around a car. Luckily, I happen to have a replacement still's got some life in her."

And with that he reached into his bag and, to my friend's utter astonishment, pulled out a used battery. In a few moments, he had installed it in the car. Chagrined, her stereotypes shot to hell, Leslie got out of the car as the stranger flagged down a passerby to help jump-start the engine. In this gift of goodness Leslie saw the soul of a fellow human being willing to put himself out for a stranger in need. Was she willing to do the same? Leslie was so moved she eventually became involved in a Skid Row effort known as the Chrysalis Center, helping people down on their luck get a hand up.

By going off the regular route of her life, Leslie had encountered a miracle of human giving that awakened meaning in her life. She became involved in the lives of others. She could see them differently, more completely, even as my journey into the Highlands of Scotland gave me a fuller picture of its majesty. It takes the same existential journey, willingness to go beyond what we've grown accustomed to, in order to truly know others and, perhaps most important, to uncover and receive the hidden beauty in ourselves. Sometimes it might just take getting off the road of life to truly see where we're going.

~

Each of us has highlands in our lives. And if we are willing to go "a wee ways beyond" there's no telling the wonders we'll receive by giving life the chance to make a second impression.

unfinished business

As we grow in years and mileage, often we can be nudged by a memory, a task uncompleted, a word never spoken.

I have a feeling that regrets can serve a useful purpose. With focus and a creative heart, we can use these nagging pieces of unfinished business to know ourselves in ways that reveal ever more colors in our life's mosaic.

The initial task is to sift and sort the regrets. Some regrets serve only to torpedo our existence, while others can knit themselves into our lives and nudge us toward redemptive acts. For example, the day you missed your daughter's big piano recital because you got caught up in the minutiae of an office problem and lost track of time—that's a tough one. Tough especially because it is all too human and all too preventable. Her tears cut so deep you thought they'd never heal. You've probably kicked yourself plenty over it, and the bruises still show. Hopefully, when things like this happen—and they do happen to all of us—we use the memory to ensure it doesn't happen again. That is the gift in the pain of missed opportunities. We can learn.

Many of us do not seize an opportunity to close a particular circle, to finish unfinished business. Perhaps we cannot find the courage needed to speak a few words, and the words are left unsaid for years, and the years that leave that regret marinating below the surface until it has transformed into a veritable stew of heartache. But then life and circumstances change, as life and circumstances invariably do, and we are ready to receive the gift of closure.

A close family friend is an extremely popular woman. Poised, talented, with a loving husband and children, she is accomplished in ways many dream of being. But she years ago latched onto a friendship with another woman who had served as a kind of mentor in her personal growth. The two had been inseparable, planning projects, sharing advice, family dinners, the good life of two people who care about each other. But slowly, the mentor began to pull away. She called less often, allowing weeks to go by between contact, and had little time for the caring personal counsel that was her hallmark. Our friend tried to change herself, to become more like the mentor in order to return to her graces. Of course, it didn't work. Finally, our friend received a note, which simply said, "We've outgrown this relationship between us. Life is full of changes. I wish you the best."

Our friend was stunned. It was painful for her husband and those of us who love her to see how deep was her sense of abandonment. With all the other doors of friendship and family open to her, our friend could see only the one closed. She felt as if some life-force had been stripped away. She pulled away, not having the strength to confront her former friend and regretting it every day.

Only with the passage of time and through growth in seeing herself positively has our friend been able to confront this unfinished business. Recently she composed a letter that outlined the patterns of their relationship—the mentor-apprentice feel of it, the different directions their lives had been going, the more public role that she, the younger of the two, had that may have caused some jealousy. She was also able to say that her life had no room for anyone who didn't want to be in it and that she understood people can fall away from each other and the world won't end. Indeed, she thanked the mentor for the gifts of their friendship and shared a prayer for the woman's own life's journey. With that, she hand-delivered the letter and, at peace with herself, moved on.

During the time that our friend was feeling so abandoned and cut off, and recognizing the dark hole of regrets in which she found herself, I wrote her the following poem. Perhaps, for any who have gone or are now going through rejection, it may shed some light on the gift you can receive with the awareness of your own inner strength:

The Way Home

We experience abandonment like a kiss from the universe
removed from the heart.

A presence and an acknowledgment have vanished, leaving
    behind the echo of what *was,*
the emptiness of what *is.*
Traveling the river of rejection, we seemingly are forced,
without benefit of oars or rudder,
to find our way back
to a happiness we once called home.

And so, for a time, we drift in search of a lifeline,
glimpsing along the way
remnants of a relationship floating by.

Observing, as if outside ourselves,
as these pieces of lost souls wash ashore
at various embankments beyond our reach.

Until the day arrives . . .
a dawning of awareness.

And we see,
perhaps more clearly than ever before,
that our lifeline was within us all the time.

And as with Dorothy in Oz,
we carry within our own hearts
the ability to take ourselves home.

In order to receive the gift of closure, and the peace of mind and heart that come with it, we need to find that place within us that bridges the river of rejection and the chasm of abandonment.

We begin to receive that gift when we see the loose strands of our lives as opportunities for personal growth, for learning from our pain. We recognize that turning ourselves into someone we're not brings neither happiness nor healing. We allow ourselves to glimpse the vision of who we want to be and who we can be. We learn that regrets over the missed chances we had in the past to speak or act need not add up to failure but can help us embrace today's opportunity for closure.

Finishing unfinished business, whenever it happens, is a celebration of our individuality. For it means we have received loud and clear the message the universe has been sending us: *we carry within our own hearts the ability to take ourselves home.*

The Miracle in Blue Pajamas

Wonder comes in all shapes and sizes, at any place and in any moment of the day.

It can emerge out of a long cry or at a family reunion. It can show its face when a sudden realization clicks as we muse over a cup of coffee, and we're propelled into action. I've seen it in Skid Row when a woman and her children get back on their feet for a second chance at life, and I've encountered it on the ballfield in the gracious sportsmanship of my eleven-year-old stepson. If you stop to consider the moments in which you've come across wonder, you recognize the aura that comes with such experiences. It's as if, once you take in the miracle of it, your next breath is a bit more sacred.

When we receive such gifts from the universe, we know the meaning of a blessing from the inside. And when they manifest as someone dear to us nears death, they seem to carry a benediction of grace.

Leo Evans was one extraordinary guy. A retired business-man, he had devoted his postemployment years to bringing laughter and learning to residents of retirement homes. He believed deeply that engaging the mind and touching the heart generate the life-force within you, no matter how old or fragile you become. Divorced for twenty-six years, living on his own, Leo had made it his personal business to bring smiles and meaning to the elderly.

Meeting Leo was a little like approaching one of those question-and-answer machines found in the old days along a boardwalk or at Coney Island. The mystical talking head offered a query or posed a brainteaser and awaited your response. Or it might engage in prognostication or sublime humor. Which was Leo in a nutshell. You never came away from the man without a riddle to solve, an anecdote to treasure, a joke to enjoy. His eyes twinkled just at the sight of you. He brought merriment to countless souls and found the magic of meaning in his gift. So it was with heavy heart that those of us who knew and loved him witnessed his pain in the final weeks of terminal cancer.

His family had been at his bedside, helping him prepare for his death, sharing stories and tears. Leo was fully alert and present in the moment. His son-in-law, Graham, my longtime friend, called one day to let me know that the end was imminent and asked me to lead a memorial service when the time came. Which set me up for the call I received a few days later. I heard Graham's voice on the line and sighed, ready to hear the sad news of Leo's death, mentally kicking myself for not having gone to see him the day before. But the call was not about death. It was not about planning a funeral or counseling a family or dealing with endings. It was nothing less than a shot of wonder across the bow of mortality.

To my utter and complete amazement, Graham asked if I was free to perform a wedding. I tried to switch gears but couldn't get the words out. How could the family be planning a wedding with the patriarch lying there near death? But the groom was to be none other than Leo himself. I was dumbfounded. The most surprising news was yet to come. The woman he had divorced those twenty-six years earlier, Joyce, had remained his friend. They had shared family celebrations with their children and grandchildren. But they had lived separate lives—until now. From the midst of his decline, Leo looked into her eyes as she sat by his bedside and held his hand in friendship until the end. In that miracle moment Leo smiled through his pain and said, "You have been my friend all these years, even after the divorce. Would you do me the honor of becoming my wife once again?"

Joyce, stunned and with tears trailing down her check, simply responded in a whisper, "Leo, you've swept me off my feet."

Which is how I found myself a day later when I entered the hospital and was instantly flanked by a coterie of well-wishers in white. Doctors, nurses, even the security guard escorted me to Leo's room for an event hospital workers don't get much of a chance to enjoy—nuptials in room 303-B.

As I approached the room, I could see the decorations the

floor nurses had hung over Leo's doorway. The staff was positively giddy—a life-affirming moment in the midst of so much pain. And then I entered the room. There he was, the groom, sitting up in a chair, tubes trailing off his arms, his characteristic twinkle in his eyes. Pulling himself up with brave demeanor, he nodded with a wry smile, "Wore my best blue pajamas."

And so, with Joyce in the chair next to him, and their granddaughter's prayer shawl for a *chuppah,* what was once divided was mended, a circle repaired, and in place of an ending, a beginning. We were all overwhelmed. Hospital personnel crowded at the door. I actually heard a doctor call out "wait a minute" when paged. It was mesmerizing. Looking into Leo's eyes, I told him what was in my heart, in all of our hearts. Even at this challenging moment, he was continuing to teach us—to remind us that life is about loving, about second chances, about holding onto friendship, about reaffirming the sacred within our lives. About fashioning blessings, yes, even on the threshold of life's completion. He was teaching us that life can be *this* good when we can be *this* human.

Those of us in the room bore witness to the gifts of the human spirit, which dares to dream in the midst of suffering. Dares to say "yes" when life says "not now." Dares to choose the grace with which to face the pain.

Leo died eleven days later, his family encircling him in a

benediction of love, his bride by his side. He had touched thousands.

And each time his story is told, his spirit continues to engage the mind and touch the heart.

～

No matter what our age, we can receive the gift of grace through approaching life in a way that affirms life. That says there are still cups of life out there to fill with the wine of human celebration. That we are, each of us, gifts of wonder, transmitters of joy through which the universe moves and shouts in gladness. And we are capable of generating and receiving the gift of that joy at the most unusual moments.

Thanks to the man in blue pajamas, I won't ever forget that.

The Human Chrysalis

Nature produces few transformations more marvelous than that of the caterpillar into a butterfly. The chrysalis effect is the name for this metamorphosis, moving from earth to air. And it is a change that carries with it both the values of community and individuality.

When the first chill of autumn signals the killing frost of the northern winter, monarch butterflies begin their migration to the south, where they seek protection and more plentiful nectar. They can travel over the Rockies and the Sierra, from as far as Canada, to cluster along the California coast in the safety of pine and eucalyptus. In a remarkable display of teamwork, the butterflies form dense clusters along the tree branches, each animal hanging, wings down over the butterfly below it, forming living shingles to shelter one another from heavy winds or storms. The weight of this group effort anchors the winged community, making it more difficult for one or more to be shaken free.

When they get around to the return flight in spring, these monarchs make quick work of it, reportedly beating their wings rapidly through a 120-degree arc, sending the cloud of butterflies along at speeds of thirty miles an hour.

Along the way eggs will be laid and larvae hatch, and caterpillars will evolve and eventually come to hang upside down from twigs and leaves. There each must use its own creative and inner resources to shed its skin and spin a protective cocoon, in which it will transform itself into an elegant creature.

Clinging to this chrysalis after it emerges, the butterfly pumps body fluid into its limp wings, causing them to expand to some sixty times their original size. And soon the migration begins anew. As one generation dies out another takes its place, radiant velvet-winged animals going about the urgent business of living.

Takes your breath away.

And in the caterpillar's transformation and the butterfly's habits are lessons about beauty and the effort required for each of us to evolve.

For we human creatures also need a community in which to flourish and find safety. The monarch butterflies strengthen one another when buffeting winds threaten them by placing their wings over their fellow. Have we not the same needs— to shelter our loved ones, family, and friends under our warmth and compassion? And do we not also need to receive a loving embrace, the kind that allows us to heal when we've been hurt, to get our bearings when the winds of life have threatened our footing?

And are there not strangers in our midst who cry out for

the same loving embrace of a community when their safety has been shaken? Each of us needs to receive the gift of a community, sometimes in the form of a close circle of loved ones, other times in the form of general human kindness.

And watch the caterpillar as it takes upon itself responsibility for its own transformation. Through its example, we may understand all the more clearly that the power to grow and change lies within us. Each of us is capable of designing our own personal development by taking the time to turn inward, drawing upon the source of creativity that helps to spin a human chrysalis. It is inside ourselves that we must look for the raw materials with which to transform into the radiant creatures we know we can be. It is an inner journey we must make, like the caterpillar, in order to find the inspiration for a human and spiritual metamorphosis.

Nature teaches us about our own abilities in so many ways if we're prepared to receive the knowledge.

Like a roaring river, we are powerful enough to move the obstacles in our course.

Like the birch tree whose bark peals away to reveal another beneath it, we are capable of shedding one layer to renew ourselves as we enter new seasons of our lives.

Like a rhapsodic rainbow, we can combine our many human colors into an arch of beauty to inspire others.

And like the simple butterfly, we can fill our wings with the ingredients necessary for our dreams to take flight.

~

When we study the world around us, we recognize that we are connected to each creature, every blade of grass, through the gift of growth and change. We see that human transformation combines the strength of community and the beauty of our individual spirit. And our challenge is to continue to evolve in concert with the universe.

In order to receive the gift of growth, we, like the caterpillar, must make that inner journey. At the end of that odyssey are the wings of our dreams, ready to bear us anywhere we want to go.

Yes, life can be *this* good.

The Exit Interview

"All beginnings are hard." That's from the Talmud. Those of us who remember the tenuous tremble of tying our shoes for the first time know its veracity. Learning to ride a bike, making new friends, changing schools or our workplace, starting over after a divorce, giving birth—beginnings are most definitely a challenge. But how about endings?

We hear regular apocalyptic warnings about the fate of the faithless and the cholesterol-crazed among us. But no one gives you a clear picture about exactly what to expect at the grand adios.

A scenario has been playing in my head for some time now. Perhaps it stems from the loss of my father years ago. Then again, it might have something to do with my becoming a midlife daddy at the same time as I enter the guild of grand-fatherhood, a convergence that tickles my friends and enriches my therapist.

From wherever this imagined interplay springs, I have been nursing a vision of the rite of passage conducted at the moment we transition from our lives. This vision has absolutely nothing to do with heaven and hell, concepts best left to those who see fear as a necessary seed to faith. Rather,

I see this transition in the guise of an accounting. An exit interview, if you will.

Picture this: at the moment of death, we are transported to a gentle, breeze-laced grove of birch trees. All right, it's my favorite setting, nestled right there among Vermont's Green Mountains. Feel free to jump in with an appropriate idyllic scene of your choice—a beach in Hawaii, the ski slopes at Aspen, atop a float in Macy's Thanksgiving Day Parade. Now, safe within our favorite setting, we are presented with a series of questions meant to hone in on the experience of the life we've just left.

Thing of it is, the universe itself conducts the postlife interview. And unlike marketing corporations that seek information to better the merchandise or message, the universe doesn't give a hoot about improving the product. Life may have its share of defects, it reasons, but life is far and away the best commodity ever mass-produced. No, what the universe wants to know in this survey—or, more precisely, wants us to focus on at this cosmic moment of truth—is this: Of all the gifts sent our way, how many did we actually "get"?

Now we might think an aptitude for business or a high IQ would impress the interviewer. But we quickly find out it all means *gornisht*. *Bupkis*. Like all those promises we made to give up chocolate. No, all that really matters at this moment and in this place is our AQ—our *awareness* quotient.

In my imagination the questions go something like this . . . .

- Do you remember the time you were sitting with your little girl at a performance of *The Nutcracker Suite,* and she looked up at you with a smile that could melt the polar icecap? You were mentally counting up the day's wins and losses on the market, but did you manage to catch even a glimpse of that incredible smile?

- The trip to Maine with the whole family. Remember the rainbow along the coast? Now that was a masterpiece, if I do say so. You were occupied with having gained a few pounds. You felt ugly and unappreciated. I put that rainbow up there just for you. Did you ever look up to see those colors?

- The day in the post office when everything had gone wrong, remember? You'd had a run-in with the boss. You were late getting your son to school. Your mother called to let you know that you hadn't called. You'd waited in a long line to mail a small package, and when you got to the postal clerk you realized you'd left your money and credit card back in the office and you'd have no time to come back and get the package reweighed, and it was a gift for your best childhood friend. As you stood there yelling in frustration, a little girl heard you. She offered you her money. She was so proud. She said someone had helped her once and she was just helping back.

I think about this exit interview and, like Dickens' Scrooge, recognize these are ghosts of things that may be but not necessarily will be. Not if we make different choices.

Each of us is an instrument in the orchestra of life, and, like the woodwinds, strings, and timpani, we are in need of periodic tuning. The tuning fork that trains us into wonder appears in the form of gifts of life sprinkled all around us every day—gifts of nature, of the spirit, and of the heart. The experiences I've shared in this book are some of the gifts that have become my personal tuning fork. They have helped make me a better instrument, more fully aware of my own possibilities. They have helped me to see how good life can be and have helped me to live it in that spirit.

Many of us, in the challenging journey of our existence, search for signs, for meaning, seeking to awaken to life's possibilities. We inquire after the miracles that can enrich our living—like the voice I heard shimmering across the waters in Scotland, urging me to listen, open, step into, and receive. Consciously or subconsciously, we are searching for these gifts through which the universe is communicating the affirmation of our humanity—indeed, our very being.

And we are sent these gifts, not in solitary measure, but in bushels:

> the artist's palette of autumn leaves
> a child's kiss
> a whisper of comfort from someone we've never met

the opportunity to finish unfinished business
Mozart
rainbows
the clasp of a friend's hand and a lover's heart
the magic of snowfall
grandchildren
sunsets

We search for miracles.
We receive . . . *Life*.

If we will *listen* with the ears of our hearts,
open our souls,
step into each day with purpose and awareness,
then we will truly *receive* the gifts
that awaken us to the certain knowledge that—
life can be *this* good.

~

Until the next time we gather around the fire,
Blessings.

ACKNOWLEDGMENTS

To create a book is to journey in search of grace. A writer carries a passion of ideas, seeking the right path to fulfill an inner promise. If you are fortunate, all along the way you find precious people who prod and inspire and challenge and support you and whose awareness helps open up your own. And in the end, the book can continue its trek beyond the arms of the author because so many have blessed its journey in wondrous ways. The gifts of their contributions bestow the grace you seek.

I am forever in the debt of the caring and passionate staff of Conari Press, who embody the very best of publishing. Leslie Berriman is wonder in action, an editor of joy and wisdom whose spirit is woven into this book. She not only helped midwife it, she enriched my soul in the process. Brenda Knight's enthusiasm and amazing talents as director of sales have been an inspiration from the beginning. She is a maker of magic. Heather McArthur as managing editor has guided me through numerous checkpoints with the graciousness that is her hallmark. Leah Russell and Julie Kessler led me through the maze of an author's book tour with a passion and commitment for which I am deeply grateful. Priscilla Stuckey—

copyeditor extraordinaire—polished the manuscript with a discerning eye. Jenny Collins, Suzanne Albertson, and Claudia Smelser have tapped their creative souls to design and produce a joyous physical look. Rosie Levy, Don McIlraith, Brian Reed, Everton Lopez, Mignon Freeman, and publisher Will Glennon round out a team that is matchless.

Arielle Ford and the Ford Group have been an integral part of the promotion of this book. I treasure not only Arielle's rich counsel but also the honor of her friendship. And Katherine Kellmeyer is simply a godsend of creative energy.

I am forever grateful to Lili and Jon Bosse, who believed in me before I began this endeavor and continue to make a difference in my family's life. A special embrace to Lili, who has been a constant light and a presence of support and affirmation throughout.

My thanks to Shirley Levine, mentor and friend, who has blessed me over the years with her heart's wisdom. And to all my colleagues at Heschel—indeed, to all who teach and ennoble the human spirit.

Gratitude to Jane Powell for continued support as well as to her late husband, my friend and role model, Charles Powell.

To so many who have blessed me with their friendship and encouraged me along the way: my thanks to Loren Judaken, David and Jocelyn Lash, Mel Powell, Debby Berger, Dirk and Linda Wassner, Stella Resnick, Rachelle Berger, Graham and Lori Becker, Judy and David Leonard, Dotty and Larry Brody, Farla and Hershey Binder, Max and Lisa Goldberg, Marion Blumenthal, Terry Rosenberg, Karen and Ken Scopp. In addition, my appreciation to Jon Voight, Senator Patrick Leahy, Debrah Constance, Sister Patricia Connor, Miriam Rivas and her family, and Fredi Friedman, whose initial comments on the manuscript were illuminating.

My deepest gratitude to Richard Carlson for his gracious spirit and incomparable heart.

My thanks to Deepak Chopra, Carolyn Rangel at the Chopra Center for Well-Being, Elie Wiesel, Cherie Carter-Scott, John Gray, Simon Wiesenthal, Debbie Ford and David Wolpe. And to my agent Linda Chester, for her hard work and ongoing plans to help put my books out into the world.

My parents, Roberta and Frank Goldstein, set me on the creative path and instilled in me a belief in myself and in tomorrow. They have always been the foundation of my life's blessings.

My sister, Ethel, and her husband, John; my brother Michael and his wife, Cheryl; my brother Mark and his wife, Kyoko; and my brother- and sister-in-law, Glenn and Linda: all of you are part of the circle of family that enriches my journey.

My mother and father-in-law, Marion and Matt Solomon, have not only assisted me with their feedback and suggestions but also inspired me to make my dreams come true. Marion, especially, has been a sounding board without whom this journey would have been much diminished.

To my sons-in-law, Andy and Chris, and my grandchildren, Asher and Isabella: you have, with the help of my daughters, introduced me to a fortunate world. You make Papa's life such a celebration.

My children, Yaffa, Batsheva, and Elisha, helped to open my awareness to the beauty of life and have been by my side through a myriad of life's challenges, blessing me with their hearts. They are integral to my soul's delight. No parent could be prouder.

My stepson, Ari, and my newborn daughter, Shira, continue the process of teaching me about the joys of fatherhood. They bring the gift of light each day.

And to my best friend, my wife, Bonnie, who believed in the soul of this book when it was simply a wish floating on the wind (and who possesses an amazing ability for transforming the "no" Life can sometimes send our way into a "yes!"). You give my dreams wings and allow me to awaken to the miracles each and every day.

For further information on Jan Goldstein, his book tour,
lectures, and workshops, please see his website:
www.JanGoldstein.com

Jan would love to hear from you if you wish to share a personal story or anecdote on how good life can be. You may
send your stories or comments about this book by emailing
them to him at Jan@jantalk.com

TO OUR READERS

CONARI PRESS publishes books on topics ranging from spirituality, personal growth, and relationships to women's issues, parenting, and social issues. Our mission is to publish quality books that will make a difference in people's lives—how we feel about ourselves and how we relate to one another. We value integrity, compassion, and receptivity, both in the books we publish and in the way we do business.

As a member of the community, we donate our damaged books to nonprofit organizations, dedicate a portion of our proceeds from certain books to charitable causes, and continually look for new ways to use natural resources as wisely as possible.

Our readers are our most important resource, and we value your input, suggestions, and ideas about what you would like to see published. Please feel free to contact us, to request our latest book catalog, or to be added to our mailing list.

2550 Ninth Street, Suite 101
Berkeley, California 94710-2551
800-685-9595 · 510-649-7175
fax: 510-649-7190
e-mail: conari@conari.com
www.conari.com